Shashi Deshpande's

That Long Silence

A Critical Study

Celebrating Indian Literature

Shashi Deshpande's

That Long Silence

A Critical Study

Santwana Haldar

abc
asia book club
an international publishing house

Published by
Asia Book Club
Post Box 9615
New Delhi 110 058
Ph. 9818755529

ISBN: 81-7851-021-9

Printed at Chaman Offset Press, New Delhi 110 002

Contents

for

Riya, who will fulfil my hopes

Introduction

Indian fiction in English has a galaxy of women novelists starting from Kamala Markandaya, a galaxy that includes among others, such widely acclaimed novelists as Nayantara Sahgal, Ruth Prawer Jhabvala, Attia Hosain, Anita Desai and Shashi Deshpande. In the changing scenario of postcolonial Indian society that observed crosscurrents of traditional ideals and newly imported ones, these women novelists were burdened with the task of giving their women characters the specific roles that would fit in the socio-cultural modes and values of the changed society. A new generation of women emerged, embracing the changed values according to which women have a voice of their own, a voice that had been suppressed for centuries. These women, who have the capacity to make free choice and need not therefore depend on the choice of the male, are portrayed in the novels of the new generation women novelists. These new women characters are not however the same everywhere: they react to the particular situation they are in, and their psychic and moral dilemmas are exposed accordingly.

The Fiction of Shashi Deshpande

Shashi Deshpande, a well known name in Indian literature in English, began her literary career in 1970, with the publication of a collection of short stories. Daughter of an eminent Kannada dramatist and Sanskrit scholar, Adya Rangacharya (Sriranga), Shashi Deshpande was born in Dharwad (in Northern India) in the year 1938. She received her graduate degree (Hons. in Economics) from Bombay and then moved to Bangalore to obtain a degree in Law. She also took a course in journalism and worked for a magazine for a brief period of time. Later, she settled in Bangalore with her family.

Shashi Deshpande's stories and novels were first published by small literary publishers like Writers' Workshop in Calcutta. But gradually her novels began to be accepted by internationally famous publishers such as Virago Press and Penguin Books. Besides four children's books, she has written novels such as *The Dark Holds No Terrors, If I Die Today, Come up and be Dead* and *Roots and Shadows* before the publication of her Sahitya Akademi Award winning novel *That Long Silence* (first published in 1988) *The Binding Vine, A Matter of Time*, *Small Remedies* and *Moving On* are her later novels which drew the critics' immediate attention. After a hard struggle for a footing in the literary world, Shashi Deshpande is now acclaimed as a representative woman writer of India all over the world. Her short story 'The Legacy' has been prescribed by Columbia University in its literature syllabus. Her works are now translated in different languages and are available in different corners of the world, particularly in the English-speaking world. It is her command over English language that contributes to her worldwide fame. But her hold on psychology, particularly female psychology, her keen observation of the changes in society and her deep knowledge of the Indian tradition are not to be underestimated.

Women Characters

Thanks to the worldwide trend of feminism, the women characters belonging to different strata of life are the centre of attraction in the novels of the women writers. Kamala Markandaya's *Nectar in a Sieve* is perhaps the first full-length study of a rural Indian woman in English. Rukmani is the representative of the poverty-stricken, hardworking, sincere and silent women of India who live like animals, embrace intolerable suffering for survival, and yet hope for a better future for their issues only to be crestfallen at the end. Nothing happens in their life but series of disappointments along with humiliation and torture and repeated displacement. Besides the rural mass, there are middle class women in the innumerable towns and cities of India who are often unable to enjoy the legal status conferred on them. Women are now treated on equal terms by law as far as inheritance of property and opportunities of job are concerned. But on the social level, these women who have been struggling since ages to assert themselves, are still being heckled by their male counterparts and forced to remain silent.

The voice of this newly emerged class of women, who have the same education as the men are having, and are sometimes given the opportunity of supporting themselves financially, is heard in the writings of the contemporary women writers. A voice of protest against the marginalized condition of women as a class is also audible in their works. The meek and submissive heroines who were accepted as the standard women characters are replaced by the bold heroines, having moral courage necessary for self-assertion. It is likely that the approach of one such enlightened woman will be different from that of others. But the common point in their approaches is distinct: the misrepresentation of women by the male writers, who always liked to render the woman as subordinate to man, is challenged.

Shashi Deshpande's approach to women's problems, as depicted in her novels, is quite distinct. It is possible to differentiate her approach from that of her contemporaries who either protest against the existing norms of the society or remain indifferent to the social system responsible for the oppression of women. Shashi Deshpande did not choose the way of protest as such, although she is loosely described as a feminist, one who is influenced by the individualistic feminism propagated by the Anglo-American feminist tradition. Deshpande's protagonists, who are educated women and most of whom are financially independent, have not necessarily developed an anti-male attitude. When one such character suffers and the husband is blamed, her father, brother or some male friend is found to be her saviour. Again, a woman is often rendered responsible for the suffering of another woman even if she is her daughter. In *The Dark Holds No Terrors* it is Sarita's mother who creates the guilt consciousness in Sarita through her hysterical accusation that Sarita had killed her kid brother Dhruva, and ultimately this repeated accusation drives her to the border of schizophrenia. In fact, Sarita desperately tried to save her dear brother Dhruva when she saw him getting drowned in a pit full of muddy water, but denied any knowledge of him out of fear when asked by her parents.

Deshpande sought to highlight Sarita's psychological condition as she was being alienated from her parents after the mishap, though she was then the only child left to her parents. The author criticizes the society that cares only for a male child and ignores the female child and fails to provide the latter a healthy atmosphere for physical and mental growth. It would be an exaggeration to hold that the sister's authority over her kid brother forms the battleground on which she was fighting for a space of her own.[1] It is quite natural for a child that he/she likes to draw full attention of the parents without which a child feels insecurity. Therefore when the parents go for a second baby they are advised not to neglect their first issue lest there be any psychological complexity. Sarita's psychological complexity was enhanced by her mother's suggestions that she should not go out into the sun and should take care of her complexion; she hated to be treated as a member of the feminine world who is supposed to take care of her feminine beauty lest she be rejected by a male for being his partner in life. This is an insult to her individuality, and she developed contempt towards femininity. She was in fact desirous of being treated as a human being, no more and no less. If others (including his male counterparts) have the freedom of moving into the sun why not she? Sarita's desire to be emancipated was fulfilled when her father, much to her mother's irritation, came forward to support her both morally and financially and she came out as a medical practitioner. It may not be full justice to Sarita and her creator to interpret all her actions as per feminist's programme. Sarita represents, as do other protagonists of Deshpande, the contemporary woman's struggle to attain an "autonomous selfhood." Sarita, Jaya (*That Long Silence*), Indu (*Roots and Shadows*), Sumi and Aru (*A Matter of Time*) and other women characters in Deshpande's novels try to assert themselves as independent individuals through confrontations with the traditional constraints in Indian society.

As the tradition demanded, the women protagonists in Deshpande's novels usually start with their roles assigned to them by the society. While other women in their surroundings appear to be happy with their roles, they cannot be happy as they have a strong urge to make a free choice for themselves. This urge is very close to an existentialist's urge for making an independent choice. A man is condemned to be free, said Sartre. And those who say that they are not free are only lying to themselves. This lying to oneself is called 'bad faith' and Sartre considers 'bad faith' to be a moral flaw.[2] The intelligent and highly conscious individuals (the women protagonists) in Deshpande's novels proceed through the hazardous way of making decisions on their own, for this is the only way to assert oneself. As it is realized by Jaya towards the end of the novel, *That Long Silence*, Lord Krishna in the *Bhagavad Gita* suggests this free choice for His devotees. To quote a few lines from the novel,

> The final words of Krishna's long sermon to Arjuna, 'Do as you desire,' I'd thought it something of a cheat. Imagine the Lord, any Master telling his disciple. . . . 'Do as you desire'! What are Prophets and Masters for if not to tell you what to do? But now I understand. With this line, after all those millions of words of instruction, Krishna confers humanness on Arjuna. 'I have given you knowledge. Now you make the choice. The choice is yours. Do as you desire.' (192)

Jaya's realization throws light on her creator's view of free choice as a moral act. After one gains full knowledge of oneself and of the way of the world, one is free to act according to one's desires. For, this time one's knowledge would act as one's guide and there is likely to be no fear on the way. An individual is expected to be true to him/her and only then preparation for free choice is complete. Broadly speaking, the protagonists in Deshpande's novels suffer on their way to getting prepared for the choice and the novels display several stages of self-realization leading to the act of choice.

The female characters in Deshpande's novels are basically Indian women; when they try to assert their individuality, emancipating from the age-old patriarchal pattern of thought, they exhibit their unique way which is sharply different from the western feminist movement. Deshpande has laid stress on the mixed cultural value systems prevalent in India and thus the indiscriminate application of western models of feminism will not do justice to her works. As Vrinda Nabar aptly comments, "The vastly different scenario in India encompasses contradictions of a kind undreamed of in the mainstream (western) feminist philosophy."[3] Thus it is almost impossible for someone, who is not accustomed to the thought pattern of the Indian middle class people, to understand how the publication of poems written by a woman long dead can cause dishonour to the family. When the central character Urmi in *The Binding Vine* is so much haunted by the poems written by her mother-in-law, who died at the time of giving birth to her son, and decides to publish the poems, a serious charge of being a traitor to the family is brought against Urmi. A slight hint at the dead woman's relation to her husband through her poems is equated to blasphemy. Hence Vanna is enraged when she comes to know that Urmi is going to publish Mira's poems. "It is as if the knowledge of what her father did, of what he was, has threatened something, disturbed the inner rhythm of her being. So that there is a sense of disharmony about her." (181) A common woman in a male-dominated society is nourished in such a way that it is impossible for her to see things from a fresh point of view, other than the male one. The traditional Indian mind fails to appreciate a poem as a work of art independent of its context. Almost a similar incident occurs when Mohan in *That Long Silence* brings the charge of infidelity against his wife who was supposed to have made public the secrets of her married life through her novels. Mohan's ego is hurt and his wife Jaya ceases to write about matters that might hurt Mohan.

Plight of an Indian Woman

Shashi Deshpande keenly observes the nature and the causes of the plight of an Indian woman writer who is suppressed both at home and in the literary world outside, in various ways. In *The Binding Vine*, Mira's diary records the conversation between Mira and the rising poet Venu who later became famous in Indian literature. Having read some of Mira's poems, Venu is reported to have said, "Why do you need to write poetry? It is enough for a young woman like you to give birth to children. That is your poetry. Leave the other poetry to us men." (127) This is the way of humiliating the other sex in the male-governed world. Whatever a woman writes is considered unnecessary, if not trash. And at home, there are psychological fears and physical sufferings along with the demand that a woman "must always be a few feet behind her husband," and in order to maintain a happy married life, she should not "try to reverse the doctor-nurse, executive-secretary, principal-teacher role." (*The Dark Holds No Terrors,* p.124) In order to assert her individuality, to be a human being in the proper sense of the term, every woman has to try hard to move beyond the barrier made for her in the society. Deshpande reveals this attempt of her protagonists in her novels and she is hardly biased against the male. That is why Urmi's husband (in *The Binding Vine*) is rendered as an ideal husband, and Urmi hardly has any dissatisfaction with her. But she has to struggle for the cause of other women in the society in order to assert her humanity.

Variety of Characters

In Deshpande's literary world there are characters taken from almost all the sections of life. There are medical practitioners and writers, educated housewives, uneducated ones and the maidservants. Besides poverty, bereavement and such other common adversities, there are some causes of suffering exclusively for the female. Deshpande renders with sympathetic understanding the variety of suffering a woman has to undergo. Sometimes the suffering is attached to the social taboos, and sometimes the woman is silenced in the name of family honour, and is compelled to digest torture. Kalpana's case in *The Binding Vine* is an example. When Kalpana is found in dying condition after she has been molested by her own relative, her mother Shakutai requests the doctor not to inform the police lest the honour of the family is gone, leaving her unable to marry her daughter off. "I'll never be able to hold up my head again," she says, "who'll marry the girl, we're decent people." (58) Urmi understands that women like Shakutai, who are rejected by their husbands and have to face the humiliation and torture, must have felt that marriage is the only shelter of a woman's life. At least one is "safe from other men." (88) This insecurity felt by the womenfolk in general puts a bar on their way to free thinking. The parents hardly encourage their female child to develop independent thinking as they are eager to get relieved of the responsibility somehow, by marrying her off. And if some parent does encourage (as does Jaya's father in *That Long Silence*), this act is hardly supported by others in the family.

Deshpande makes the social system responsible for the sufferings of women, and this system includes its female members too, who have been moulded by the society and are rendered unable to think otherwise. The anguish of the soul, weakened by unthinkable humiliations and physical torture, may be revealed by one who has direct knowledge of that anguish and a hold on language necessary for revealing that experience. Shashi has the capacity to delve deep into the anguish that eats into the very core of life, and hence she can create life-like characters like Sulu. Sulu (in *The Binding Vine*) has no other way but to give Kalpana the proposal of marrying her husband Prabhakar, as desired by him. And when Kalpana refused, and as a result was raped by Prabhakar, Sulu had no option but to commit suicide as the poor soul could no more disgrace herself by telling a lie to save her husband. Sulu's suicide throws light on the dark chapter of keeping the women silent in Indian society—a society that remains blind to its male members turned into wanton animals, possessed by lust.

Shashi Deshpande's sincere attempt to break the silence of women has been widely acclaimed in home and abroad. Her clear understanding of human relationships, her close observation of the way of the world, her unbiased attitude to dogmas and movements and her hold on English language explain her success.

NOTES

1. Sarita's childhood jealousy that becomes evident in her pushing Dhruva from her father's lap when he was hardly a year old, may not be interpreted in terms of what some critics say her "contestation with the male power." However, Sarita enjoyed the opportunity of exercising power over her little brother:

> Just three years between them. But what immense advantage those three years gave her. She had ruled over him completely. No dictatorship could have been more absolute. (35)

It is a mutual and quite natural relationship between a yonger brother and his elder sister. Dhruva was completely loyal to his sister, and always ran after her and their relationship may not be seen as Sarita's "battleground" on which she is fighting for a space of her own.

2. According to Jean-Paul Sartre, man is condemned to be free, but this freedom being unbearable, man escapes freedom of choice and seeks comfort of excuses. This state of pretending that one is not free to choose for oneself, is called "bad faith." Sartre described "bad faith" as "lying to oneself":

   > To be sure, the one who practises bad faith is hiding a displeasing truth or presenting as truth a pleasing untruth. Bad faith then has in appearance the structure of falsehood. (*Being and Nothingness*, trans. Hazel E. Barnes, p. 49)

3. *Caste as Woman* (Penguin India, 1995), p. 26.

The Story of *That Long Silence*

That Long Silence is the story of its protagonist Jaya who belonged to a middle class family in North-West India, a family that was not ready to give equal status to man and woman. Thanks to her father, who had married against the wish of his family and lived in a separate house, Jaya and her brothers were educated in a convent school and Jaya could develop her individuality under the indulgence of her father. It was her father who gave her the name 'Jaya' that means 'winner.' He had very high opinion about her daughter and would try his best to inspire her with his conviction that Jaya was not like others and that Jaya must shine in life.

> 'You are not like the others, Jaya,' Appa had said to me, pulling me out of the safe circle in which the other girls had stood, girls who had performed 'pujas' and come to school with turmeric-dyed threads round their wrists and necks, girls who, it had seemed, asked for nothing more than the destiny of being wives and mothers. While I, Appa had said, and I had agreed, would get the Chatfield Prize, or the Ellis Prize, go to Oxford after my graduation. . . . 'You are going to be different from others, Jaya,' Appa had assured me. (136)

It was bad luck for Jaya that her father expired at an early age when she was yet to be a graduate and her father's death was an inexpressible sense of sorrow for her. She had never developed a friendly relationship with her mother who was often cross with her husband and so she preferred continuing in hostel, friendless in her bereavement, to staying with her mother who hardly felt the loss of her husband.

> But Ai? How can she sit there so coolly packing up as if she does not care that Appa is dead, as if going to Ambegaon will make it better? I'm not going to Ambegaon, I'm not, she cannot make me. . . . I was crying loud, the wooden pillar rough and rasping as I ran my hands up and down it; there was a piercing point of pain as a sliver of wood entered my palm. (137)

Jaya's mother had learnt to live without her husband and after her husband's death she went back to her parental house at Ambegaon, as if her twenty years with her husband in Saptagiri had been only an interlude. Jaya being known as her father's child, her mother hardly tried to be friendly with her. Jaya was however conscious of the fact that her relationship with her father did in no way affect her life. As she said, "damn Freud for foisting our fathers on us all our lives." (150)

As it was quite natural in that situation, Jaya's relations persuaded her elder brother to marry her off at the earliest opportunity to complete the unfinished job of his father. And it was a coincidence that Jaya was selected by Mohan as his bride who could satisfy Mohan's special liking for a convent educated girl. Mohan was an engineer in a steel plant and Jaya was persuaded to believe that to reject such a groom would be sheer madness. Jaya did not object to the proposal and got married. At the time of marriage she was given a new name 'Suhasini'; and surprisingly, her personality got changed after marriage.

She found that in Mohan's home, a woman's work was sharply differentiated from a man's work. A man was never to sew or to mend or to cook even for his own sake. At first, Jaya could not follow the norms of her in-laws's home, but it took no time to get used to everything. And Jaya began to be happy when she was praised for her cooking and would feel ashamed if there was any flaw in her work. She tried to be a perfect housewife; as she said, "ever since I got married, I had done nothing but wait. Waiting for Mohan to come home, waiting for the children to be born, for them to start school, waiting for them to come home, waiting for the milk, the servant, the lunch-carrier man." (30) During the early years of their marriage, Jaya was so much attached to Mohan that she was not ready to be separated from him even for a moment. But gradually, a vacuum was created between them or rather, the halo having gone the hard reality was visible.

However, Jaya's creative self revealed itself in her attempts to write stories. When her realistic story of man-woman relationship won a prize, Mohan was critical, for, according to him, Jaya had disclosed their personal relationship to the world, dishonoring thereby the sacred vows of marriage. Jaya was crestfallen at this accusation, but she could very well understand that Mohan was unable to distinguish between art and life as he had no artistic sense in him.

> I had known then that it had not mattered to Mohan that I had written a good story, a story about a couple, a man who could not reach out to his wife except through her body. For Mohan it mattered that people might think that the couple was us, that the man was him. To Mohan, I had been no writer, only an exhibitionist. (144)

In order to keep up their relationship smooth, Jaya stopped writing realistic stories and tried her hand, instead, at imaginary incidents of a housewife's life under the pseudo name 'Seeta.' Surprisingly, Mohan liked those stories and even began to take pride in her wife's calibre as a writer. The stories under the 'Seeta' column were appreciated by the public and Jaya became famous as a woman writer. But Jaya was not happy inwardly; she knew that her Seeta column had nothing to do with reality or with her real self. Jaya could freely discuss about her stories only with Kamat, a widower, who lived alone in a flat in the building where her elder brother owned one and with whom she had earlier been acquainted. And it was Kamat who allowed her to use his address for mailing her stories. Mohan had no idea then of her attempts at story writing. Kamat had always returned her rejected stories and had given necessary advice for writing better stories. Jaya could disclose any of her problems to him—the problems which others failed to understand. After her father's sad demise she came to this man who had consoled her. Whenever she felt any problem thereafter, she would go to Kamat to get back her strength. Kamat called the Seeta column an 'obnoxious creation,' and told that Jaya was meant for something higher.

A drift in Jaya's relationship with Mohan ran parallel with her struggle with herself for coming out of the disguise of Seeta. It was gradually revealed to her that Mohan was basically self-centred and that he hardly bothered about morality particularly when his selfish interest was at stake. He did not like to help others if there was no hope of getting return. That is why he opposed Jaya's proposal of taking the responsibility of Kusum's treatment. Kusum was a niece of her aunt Vanitamami who being childless adopted Kusum, a meek and mild girl. Kusum was married off and after she failed to give birth to a male child, she developed crack and it was necessary to make arrangement for her treatment. On Vanitamami's request Jaya wanted to bring Kusum with her but Mohan rejected the idea. This time Jaya did not obey him and made arrangement for Kusum in her brother's flat in Dadar that had been presented to Jaya. It is another story that Kusum could not stay there for long and went to her husband's home where she committed suicide. However, Jaya felt that she had the capacity to exercise her influence on her husband, though she did not much like to control her husband in the way some dominating women do.

The story of Jaya and Mohan reached its climax when it was disclosed that Mohan had to go on leave as there were some serious allegations of business malpractice against him and those allegations were to be investigated. Mohan did not like to stay in their costly apartment at Churchgate for the time being, and the

Dadar flat which had once been inhabited by mad Kusum, became their refuge. Their son Rahul and daughter Rati had gone on a holiday trip accompanied by their old friends. And thus the couple got the opportunity to leave their Churchgate flat without explaining the causes of leaving it to their children. The Dadar flat was indeed a very small place for a person like Mohan who was used to costly life-style. For Jaya the situation was quite unthinkable. She could never imagine that such an immoral act could be done by her husband. Moreover, she had to face the queries in the eyes of her neighbours and maidservants. Quite naturally, Jaya remained silent and her silence was misinterpreted by Mohan who thought that Jaya was accusing him for the discomfort. Mohan angrily said that whatever he had done was meant for Jaya and the children. He explained how he had to make his boss happy for getting a good quarter and for getting transferred. And all this was for Jaya's comfort.

The rude shock that Jaya received from Mohan shook her very existence. And this shock compelled her to make a self-analysis. She felt that she had been wrong for remaining silent about Mohan's activities. She never questioned his ways, never argued with him, as she felt that Mohan was keen on doing what he had intended to do. Her self-analysis revealed her own flaws and she gradually prepared herself for facing the reality. Comparing herself with the well-known mythical figure Sita, Jaya finds that her role in life had been like that of Sita who always obeyed her husband without any question. Having analysed all her past activities, she understood, "Self-revelation is a cruel process. The real picture, the real 'you' never emerges. Looking it is as bewildering as trying to know how you really look. Ten different mirrors show you ten different faces." (1) She also found that "the ghost most fearful to confront is the ghost of one's own self." (13) In the solitude of the Dadar flat where life did not follow the daily routine—Mohan was to stay at home and the children were not there to draw attention—Jaya had enough time for self-analysis. As she sat with her pen and paper, Mohan thought that she was trying the Seeta column, having little idea that both Seeta and Suhasini had died and a new self of Jaya was on its way to emerge. As it was quite natural about the worn-out relationship, there was total misunderstanding between the two. Jaya attempted to sketch a picture of that time:

> Each relationship evolves its own vocabulary. Ours had been that of the workaday world. The vocabulary of love, which I had thought would come to us naturally and inevitably, had passed us by; so too had the vocabulary of anger. (116)

A serious quarrel broke out, or it was an angry outburst of Mohan who armed himself with an anger that seemed not quite real, but Jaya could sense a genuine hostility in his approach. He accused her of not caring about the children, of isolating herself from him and his concerns. Jaya's feeble defences had no chance before his fierce onslaught. As he told that he had allowed her to have her way in most things letting her do what she wanted, Jaya retorted: "Except when it inconvenienced you." (120) Mohan could not digest these words and challenged Jaya who had many things to say but could hardly utter any word.

> The job I wanted to take, the baby I wanted to adopt, the anti-price movement I'd wanted to take part in. . . . But, even as I listed these to myself, it came to me that perhaps it had nothing to do with Mohan, the fact that I had not done these things, that I had left them alone. Perhaps I had not really cared enough about these things myself. Instead I said, and my voice sounded sullen even to me, 'I've done everything you wanted me to.'
>
> And now, I thought, I must add: "I've sacrificed my life for you and the children." But real bitterness clawed its way through this self-mockery, and I was conscious of having been chained to his dream. (120)

But Mohan could not be stopped. And suddenly Mohan's face reminded Jaya of Rahul's when as a child he would cry after the milk bottle was pulled out of his mouth, and she could not help laughing loudly. This was like adding fuel to the fire and Mohan, blind with anger, left the flat without telling anything.

> I had to control myself, I had to cork in this laughter. But it was too late. I could not hold it any longer. Laughter burst out of me, spilled over, and Mohan stared at me in horror as I rocked helplessly. When finally I recovered myself I was alone in the room. Silence flowed into it. I wiped my face and tried to realize what I'd done. (122)

Jaya's misfortune took a complete turn after she was left alone in the Dadar flat, exposed to the neighbours' curiosity. Jaya even compared her condition to that of Kusum and pitied herself. "Hadn't she taken the biggest decision of all, the only decision that mattered in life—whether to live or to die? It could not possibly be 'poor Kusum'; it was poor Jaya." (127) However, Jaya came back to her senses trying her best to get a grip on herself. Applying her knowledge of Mohan she came to the conclusion that he had not left her, that he would come back. But she had something more to increase her anxiety and fear. She received the message that Rahul had left the company of those persons with whom he and Rati had gone out. She could not trace Rahul in the relations' places and was out of her senses. Her neighbours took care of her then and tried their best to cure and console her. When her neighbour and friend Mukta asked her when Mohan was returning, she replied that perhaps he had left her. Jaya told her, "I've failed him. He expected something from me, from his wife, and I've failed him. All these years I thought I was Mohan's wife; now he tells me I was never that, not really." (185)

It was quite natural for Mukta, who had known Kamat and had seen Jaya having relationship with Kamat, to think that Mohan must have suspicion about Kamat. But Jaya made it clear to Mukta that Kamat was never an issue in their case. Then came another revelation from Mukta who now accused Jaya of leaving

Kamat alone the day he had died. Mukta had seen her go up to his apartment that day and also heard her come down. And when she went up a little later, he was dead. Some months before he died he had told Mukta that he had had a heart attack and also gave her a key of his room providing her instructions in case of eventualities. This revelation filled Jaya's mind with repentance. She remembered how Kamat tried to hold her hand and she just ran away leaving him alone, with no apprehension of his imminent death. "The loneliness of a man facing his death—is there anything like it in this world? His pain filled this room and we could both of us feel it, Mukta and I." (186)

There was however no tragic incident in Jaya's life. Rahul had gone to his father's ancestral home at Saptagiri and along with his paternal uncle Vasant came back to Jaya after being assured that Mohan was not in the spot and that she was staying in Dadar. Mohan also sent a telegram with the message 'All well' which signifies that he was out of his problem in the office and that they were soon going to stay in their Churchgate apartment. Outwardly, therefore, the story has a happy ending: the problems of the protagonist are somehow removed and she is supposed to return to her initial condition. But inwardly, there was a drastic change in the protagonist's attitude to life.

> The knowledge of what had happened to us was terrifying. Even if Mohan came back, even if this trouble blew over, could we go back to being what we were? Something had been lost, only an illusion may be, but its loss had left such a rent in our lives that it seemed impossible for us to be able to mend it so that nothing showed. And yet I knew no life but this one. (182)

Jaya the protagonist has no faith in afterlife. Nor is she a supporter of any particular party. She is a writer in the truest sense of the word and the novel records her self-analysis. The novel also contains her assertion that she would start a new life, making an end of her long silence. She was like Sita who never questioned her husband; and now she had decided to take up the role of Maitreyee who wanted to question everything and even challenged her husband. The novel ends with Jaya's assertion that she will start a new life with her husband:

> Mohan will be back. 'All well' his telegram says. Does he mean by this that we will go back to being 'as we were.' Does it mean that, now that Mohan has sorted out his problem, and no longer fears prosecution, joblessness and disgrace, we can go back to our original positions?
>
> But it is no longer possible for me. If I have to plug that 'hole in the heart.' I will have to speak, to listen, I will have to erase the silence between us. (192)

Narrative Technique in *That Long Silence*

Shashi Deshpande displays great skill in her narrative art. *That Long Silence* is perhaps the best example of her narrative skill. The novel combines flashback method along with direct description of present incidents. Briefly speaking, the theme of the novel is the self-realization of its protagonist, a woman writer who won some fame as a contributor to a woman's magazine but later chooses to change her outlook. The novelty of the theme, its difference from a saga of chronological incidents, demanded new technique and new approach to narration. Deshpande adopted the method of describing through first person introducing, however, some changes: the protagonist seeks to express her experiences not chronologically, but as they flash during the moments of intensity preceding her free choice. The conventional technique of narration is not adequate to communicate the internal web and flow of a modern writer's (the protagonist's) psyche. Like Virginia Woolf, Shashi Deshpande believes that the novelist must remain detached from life while exposing him/her to life. Jaya, the protagonist in *That Long Silence,* practises this detachment and this practice also affects her narration.

Story Narration in *That Long Silence*

Though written in an unconventional way focusing on the interior region of Jaya's mind, *That Long Silence* covers a period of time in the external world; it starts with the outer incident of an official investigation into the business malpractice of Mohan, Jaya's husband, and ends with an assurance that Mohan has nothing to get worried. During the time of investigation, Mohan was advised to vacate his apartment and the couple shifted to the small suburban Bombay flat that had been gifted to Jaya by her brother. The children were already sent on a tour with another family, and this saved Jaya and Mohan from explaining to the children why they were going to stay in the small flat for some days. Left alone, the couple passed the worst ever days of their life, anticipating a grim future of disreputation and loss of job.

Jaya is haunted by memories of the past, her sense of failure as a writer and frustrations in their seventeen-year-old marriage weighing heavily on her. Disappointed with what he explains as his bad luck, and hurt by Jaya's silence that he interprets as her lack of concern for his job, Mohan leaves the flat without telling Jaya anything about his whereabouts. Lastly, however, it is learnt from his letter that the trouble in the office is gone and they will very soon return to their apartment. On the materialistic plane, the end of the novel may be described in terms of Mohan's good luck that saves him from scandal and loss of job. In fact, Mohan takes the matter as such; but the novel centres on Jaya's sensibilities. During her brief stay in the small flat Jaya has to encounter both her past that comes to her in the form of memory, and her present in the form of rude shock received from Mohan's accusation that his malpractice was due to Jaya's and her children's comfort. Mohan's accusation makes her face the hard reality about herself. She has to acknowledge to herself that her role as Mohan's wife has been a passive one and that she has chosen to remain silent on Mohan's activities including his moral laxity, only to keep her detached from real life. To remain silent on those issues implies her lack of proper moral sense. All these are howevei only hinted at, not directly stated. Deshpande's superb narrative technique compels the reader to follow the protagonist as she exposes herself—the claustrophobia of her childhood, the pangs received from her father's early death, the imbalance in marriage, disappointment in her two teenage children, and also her inability to write what she sought to write. The readers are required to grasp the fact that Jaya, the mother of two teenagers, is also at heart a student of seventeen, partaking of the problems and nature of the literary and mythical figures, yet to find the right track as a serious writer. Her relationships with others as exposed through her recollections of the past which includes apparently trivial matters—the past is often recollected through the techniques of complex *leitmotiv* and verbal associations—are helpful in delving deep into her mind. A brief account of the four parts of the novel will make an easy assessment of Deshpande's narrative art.

Part I

Part 1 starts with a reflection that highlights the protagonist's present state of mind:

> To achieve anything, to become anything, you've got to be hard and ruthless. Yes, even if you want to be a saint, if you want to love the whole world, you've got to stop loving individual human beings first. And if they love you, and they bleed when you show them you don't love them, not specially, well, so much the worse for them! There is just no other way of being a saint. Or a painter. A writer. (1)

Jaya wants to be a writer, not just the one meant for a Women's journal. She had already gained a little fame as a typical woman writer who wrote about girls, destined to be mated themselves with the right men. That was not the real picture of life, she now admits. And yet she projected that picture, because she was afraid to face the disturbances caused by genuine pictures of life.

The novel displays the process of Jaya's self-analysis and self-recognition that help her to emerge from her cosy corner that she had so long preferred to reality. As she reflects, "Self-revelation is a cruel process. The real picture, the real 'you' never emerges. Looking for it is as bewildering as trying to know how you really look. Ten different mirrors show you ten different faces." (1) She knows that in order to be a successful writer she has to detach her experience from her awareness of that experience, and then it may be possible for her to render a real picture of life.[1] She equates the process to that of childbirth when one is afraid because one has to lose control over one's own body. In her attempt to write about her married life too, Jaya is afraid and feels like losing control over her. She is also puzzled to find out how much of the facts of her life would be relevant in the long run. She remembers how she once reduced her bio-data to three lines recording her birth, her father's death, her marriage, the birth of two children and abortion of the third issue. Other incidents appeared irrelevant. As the novel is written in first person, it is difficult for the writer to select the relevant incidents from the protagonist's life which would highlight the crisis of her inner being that leads her towards a choice of her own. It is interesting to see how the novelist constructs the structure of narration choosing incidents from the protagonist's life, juxtaposing the present happenings with the past ones.

The second section of part one starts with a reflection on the pseudo-Puritanism of the time after Gandhi's death. Jaya recalls how his father despised her addiction to film songs—'that disgusting mush,' he would call—and had tried his best to wean her from the habit of listening to Rafi and Lata and to make her love Paluskar and Faiyaz Khan instead. The shame that she felt then survived long. While going to cinema hall, she was afraid to tell Mohan that she liked to see from the very beginning, not missing even the ads, lest she be ridiculed. But she tried frantically to get there on time, getting the kids ready for going out. That she developed almost a detached view of life is clear from her recollection:

> The kid with the endearing moustache of milk; the tender, smiling mother rubbing Vicks on her son's chest; the even younger mother feeding her baby with Farex; the brother and sister running hand in hand to adoring, smiling parents and chocolates—I loved them all. Those cosy, smiling, happy families in their gleaming home spelt

> sheer poetry to me. For me, they were the fairy tales in which people 'live happily ever after.' (3)

This description suggests that Jaya developed the art of looking at her activities from a distance from the very beginning. She is now required to add fearlessness and, if required, ruthlessness to her detachment in order to express the reality experienced by her.

Remembrances of things past are followed by the description of Jaya's arrival at the Dadar flat ten days ago. And the reason behind that coming is exposed, gradually, through several recollections. Jaya recalls how she desired a catastrophe or a disaster, not of course a personal one, in order to get relieved of the boredom and monotony of life.[2] But it was beyond her imagination that her long cherished longing for disaster would come true in the form of her husband's being entangled in a scam case, that he would be on the verge of losing his job, bringing an unimaginable hardship to all in the family. Jaya took it for granted that people like them would continue living in the way they have been accustomed to. She thought that life would "go on for us as before, punctuated by dreary quarrels, the children's successes and failures, their estrangement from each other, from us, our resentment and bitterness, old age for us, perhaps widowhood for me—this was our future. Nothing else was possible for people like us." (4-5)

The phrase 'people like us' brings, through associations, Mohan's story of some decent children and their mothers who were seen squatting on the bare ground, holding placards and demanding justice much to the indifference of all. Mohan could learn later that those were the family members of some military officers who had been arrested overnight due to security reasons without being allowed to meet their families. Mohan was horrified to see the plight of those well-educated persons. And in her imagination Jaya now includes her and her children to the line of those decent-looking persons squatting for justice. Her fear that

Mohan too might be sacked or even jailed for the charge of malpractice brought against him, led her to recollect the incident that Mohan once described with much concern. For both of them 'people like us' means, "well-educated, hard-working people in secure jobs, cushioned by insurance and provident funds, with two healthy, well-fed children going to good schools." (5)

Mohan has not been known as a kind-hearted man much concerned with the suffering humanity. What led him to describe the plight of those people—'people like us'—was his apprehension that persons belonging to the higher class in the society were also vulnerable. When Mohan described the plight of the families of the military men, he exclaimed, "How could those men have done such a thing! . . . Imagine putting your family in such a situation. It seems totally irresponsible to me." (6) Now that Mohan is reported to have done almost a similar crime, Jaya likes to remind him of his words, but she does not as she cannot become rude to him. Her approach has been like that of a trodden worm, she feels. And then she recalls a post-wedding ceremonial game in which she won over Mohan and the women in Mohan's family told that she would rule her husband at home. This matters nothing, she observes and holds that theirs has been "a delicately balanced relationship, so much so that we have even snipped off bits of ourselves to keep the scales on an even keel." (7) Jaya uses the metaphor of a pair of bullocks yoked together to explain their mutual relation and this metaphor is repeatedly used. The very image suggests compulsion and the relationship appears to be mechanical.

Coming back from the world of the past Jaya ventures to describe their arrival in the Dadar flat, an incident that took place seven days ago, and says, "It was an eerie sensation I had while climbing up the stairs with him, as if there was for that one infinitesimal moment a pause in my being, and I, detached from my self, saw this . . . a pair of bullocks yoked together." (7) The image of the bullocks also suggests silence that they have maintained so long. Keeping her detached from the scene, Jaya tries to describe how she and Mohan (the man and the woman) climbed the dingy stairs of a drab building in the heart of Bombay, met the maidservant Nayana, and how ignoring Mohan, 'the woman' unlocked the door. And at this point she fails to detach herself from what she describes, and recognizes the fact that she and Mohan are two persons having distinctness of their own and not just two bullocks yoked together. Mohan is by nature indifferent to others and now fear has been added to his indifference, leaving him a sad, obsessed man reconciled to failure, almost resembling a character in Graham Greene. Criticizing herself honestly, Jaya comes to the conclusion that she has been continuing the guerrilla warfare for many years, offering subtle resistance to Mohan and it was often through silence.

Ironically, however, Mohan hardly understood the implication of her silence, but it mattered little to her. This time it is taken seriously by Jaya when Mohan brought the charge that whatever he had done was meant for his family. He said, "It was for you and the children that I did this. I wanted you to have a good life, I wanted the children to have all those things I never had." (9) Jaya knows very well that Mohan is telling a lie, that he lacks the necessary courage to face the reality, and for the first time her mind is filled up with anger.[3] When Mohan told her that there would be an enquiry and that Agarwal was the real culprit who was now going to be finished along with Mohan, Jaya listened to him with a faint sense of bewilderment. Jaya felt that contracts, tenders, favours, commissions and such other words had nothing to do with her life and she kept mum. Mistaking her silence for accusations, Mohan bursts out: "I did it for you, for you and the children." A good many ideas and memories crowded in on her. She visualizes a picture of committing suicide— the four of them, roped together, walking into the sea. And then she understands the absurdity of the situation: "Could we have come to such a decision without squabbling? We who could not even decide upon a meal or a movie without bickering—could we have chosen death in such harmony?" Moreover, the death wish, the lemming drive, is unknown to him. Jaya yet is not so sure about his motives. "Surely there comes a moment in every human's life when he or she says, like the Sibyl—I wish to die." (11)

Mohan is however optimistic and he decides to stay in the Dadar flat to make himself unavailable for the time being. And it was taken for granted that Jaya was to follow him. Jaya recalls, "I remember now that he had assumed I would accompany him, had taken for granted my acquiescence in his plans. So had I. Sita following her husband into exile, Savitri dogging Death to reclaim her husband, Draupadi stoically sharing her husband's travails." (11) That these roles of mythical women would only render her a fool, is known to Jaya who again uses the metaphor of the bullocks yoked together to describe their position. "Two bullocks yoked together . . . it is more comfortable for them to move in the same direction. To go in different directions would be painful; and what animal would voluntarily choose pain?" (12) To emerge from the existence of an animal at the cost of pain and to make a choice on her own becomes her preoccupation in the Dadar flat after she is rudely shocked by Mohan's accusation that she too is indirectly involved in the scam. (He did it all for her and the children, he said.) For Jaya the only way out is an encounter with reality and to express that reality through her writing. Whatever she wrote so far was not the expression of her real self but her poses.

So that Jaya is eager to face her real self, she has to face the real past which she calls 'ghosts.' As she enters the Dadar flat, the 'ghosts' sprang out at her: "Makarandamama, Ai, Dada and his friends, Rahul, a small, excited child, . . . All these people seemed so real to me that I looked at Mohan wondering whether he could see them too." (12) But Mohan is too materialistic to see any 'ghost.' He is unable to take moral responsibility for his work and seeks comfort in the plea that he misappropriated for his family. His lack of moral sense (that brings order in one's inner being), is compensated by his fastidiousness, his passion for neatness and order which seemed amazing to Jaya. When the couple enters the flat, Mohan becomes intolerant with the untidy place and they start cleaning and putting things in order. Left alone, Jaya gets the idea that "the ghost most fearful to confront is the ghost of one's old self." (13) And her past is visualized in a detached way. She sees her past activities as if she were some other person:

> This was what I saw, the ghost of a woman who had scrubbed and cleaned and taken an inordinate pride in her achievements, even in a toilet free from stains and smells. (13)

This woman is a ghost of Jaya, for Jaya has by now deviated from this earlier self of her. And this meeting the earlier self is like having a stranger thrusting upon oneself, claiming a relationship that is denied. That earlier self which developed after her marriage is better identified by the name 'Suhasini' given to her by Mohan at the time of marriage. And Suhasini, distinct from Jaya, was a "soft, smiling, placid, motherly woman," one who lovingly nurtured her family and who knew how to cope. Now that Jaya has left behind 'Suhasini,' she is able to criticize the type of 'Suhasini' as being selfish and cruel. She equates 'Suhasini' to the sparrow in the bed-time story of the crow and the sparrow. In that story the poor crow, shivering and sodden, went to sparrow's home for shelter. The sparrow kept the crow waiting for a long time and finally when it lets the crow in, it advises the crow to warm itself on the hot pan. The foolish, improvident, gullible crow sat on the hot pan and was burnt to death. Jaya was horrified with the sadistic tale that was told to children. Later she found that the story carried a dreadful moral: the survivor is the sparrow who is cautious, self-centred, worldly wise, dutiful and shrewd. In the guise of providing sympathy and shelter, the sparrow kills the crow. And it does all this for its safety and security. Surprisingly, the victim in the story, the crow, is a male and the victorious sparrow a female. But Deshpande wants to show that the sparrow is the ultimate loser, because there is no such thing as safety and the female cannot be safe even if she is devoid of all moral values for the sake of maintaining her family safe. Equating 'Suhasini' to the sparrow in the story, the writer lays bare the inhumanity and deceitfulness of the traditional role of woman as a mother and a housewife, a role glorified by the society and accepted by the gullible women folk:

> I have a feeling that even if little boys can forget this story, little girls never will. They will store this story in their subconscious, their unconscious or whatever, and eventually they will become that damnably, insufferably priggish sparrow looking after their homes, their babies . . . and to hell with the rest of the world. Stay at home, look after your babies, keep out the rest of the world, and you're safe. That poor idiotic woman Suhasini believed in this. I know better now. I know that safety is always unattainable. You're never safe. (17)

This realization of Jaya is the first step towards her self-recognition and the completion of the process will be marked by her free choice as a writer.

The stories behind the equation of the sparrow in the story and a woman like Suhasini are gradually revealed through Jaya's recollections. She recalls the unfortunate woman Kusum, a distant relation of hers, whom she sheltered in the Dadar flat despite Mohan's antipathy towards her.[4] Mohan said,

> Why do you want to burden yourself with her? She is not your responsibility, is she? And it is not that she's related to you, either. . . . I'm not being unreasonable. Have I ever come in the way of your helping any of your people? I've always allowed you to do what you want. But this woman isn't just sick, she's mentally sick. Is it wise to have her at home? Think of the children. (19)

'The children' have always been their final argument, their justification for everything. And Jaya was defeated. But she argued that Kusum should be kept in the Dadar flat, away from the children and Kusum began to stay there despite Mohan's contempt. Not only Mohan but also Jaya's two brothers and her mother opposed the idea of taking Kusum's responsibility. Yet Jaya stuck to her decision though her sincerity could not save the poor woman who was reported to have committed suicide. Jaya's silent struggle against the limitations imposed on her by her husband and also by other members of her family is thus recalled by her. She is also aware that such scattered cases of silent revolt are not enough for asserting her individuality. She began to prepare her internally for making a fresh ground as a writer.

Shashi Deshpande's narrative art depends on juxtaposing the past with the present through natural ways of associations in the process of memory. After their entry into the Dadar flat, Mohan notices the picture of lord Ganesh on the calendar being smeared with vermillion and is surprised. Jaya says that it must have been Kusum who was missing her gods during her stay in the flat and substituted the calendar with a photograph of lord Ganesh on it for her god, and worshipped it. This reference to Kusum opened the bylanes of memory in quite a natural way and Kusum's story, a typical one in Indian background, is rendered as Jaya's past experience. Isolated, significant moments in experience with which Jaya is concerned as a human being, are described quite naturally, without confusing the readers' minds. And then, after the story of Kusum is told, Jaya comes back to the present and goes on projecting snaps from their life in the Dadar flat. The couple followed the routine of drinking tea, taking bath and such other bare necessities of life and then did not know what to do with the rest of time.

> It was not the larger conundrum of what we were to do with our lives that confronted us; it was a simpler puzzle—what are we to

> do with ourselves this moment, this day, the next moment, the next day. . . .
>
> But there was no answer to the question. It seemed to be flung into an abyss. Nothing returned, not even an echo. . . .
>
> The truth was that we had both lost the props of our lives. Deprived of his routine, his files, his telephone, his appointments, he seemed to be no one at all; certainly not that man, my husband, around whose needs and desires my own life revolved. There was nothing he needed, so there was nothing for me to do, nothing I had to do. My own career as a wife was in jeopardy. The woman who had shopped and cooked, cleaned, organized and cared for her home and her family with such passion . . . where had she gone? We seemed to be left with nothing but our bodies, and after we had dealt with them we faced blankness. The nothingness of what had seemed a busy and full life was frightening. (24-25)

Here is a commanding voice of narration that arrests the reader's attention immediately and exposes the internal crisis: the protagonist not only suffers from a loss of personality but faces a dichotomy between the body and the soul.

It is curious to note that despite the feeling of uneasiness attached to suffering, Jaya has a sense of freedom that she has nothing to cleanse or to arrange in the household. The 'monsters' that ruled her life so long—gadgets that had to be kept in order, the glassware that had to sparkle, the furniture and the curios that had to be kept spotless and dust-free, and the clothes that had to be washed—have now vanished, leaving her enough time to deal with. She is surprised that she thinks of them in terms of monsters, for it was she who hankered after those objects. The fact becomes clear to her that she could not choose for herself, but only made her fit for the kind of life Mohan wanted to lead, and that too, in an unconscious way, without analyzing herself to know if she had desired any other mode of existence. This time also when she feels free, she does not know what she wants. She only knows that the bareness and ugliness of the place pleased her more than their carefully furnished home in Churchgate, and that she had a queer sense of homecoming when she entered the flat with Mohan. This sense implies that her efforts to run a happy family were not prompted by her genuine will. It was her surrounding, her society, that moulded her thoughts, rendering her unable to exercise her free will. Her sense of freedom in the Dadar flat is the first step towards her self-recognition.

The technique of revealing the past through association is used again when Jaya feels that it is as if she were in her Saptagiri ajji's home. The reference to Saptagiri ajji (her father's mother) takes her back to her childhood days when she would go to Saptagiri, her father's ancestral home. Saptagiri ajji was a representative of traditional Hindu widow observing penitence. She denuded herself of all those things that make up a woman's life. She had no possession except two saris she wore. She would sit on bare ground and slept on a straw mat at night. Jaya's father lived in a separate house and everyday he would go to Saptagiri to see his mother, and at that time Jaya would accompany him. She liked to be in the outside sitting room which looked like a museum with all its furniture unchanged. The recollection of Saptagiri ajji's remark that Jaya would be a disturbing factor for her husband because of her nature—she had question for everything and also retort for everything, ajji said—brings Jaya back to the present again. She says that she has neither any question nor any retort for Mohan now, and yet there is no comfort. The silence seems heavy with uneasiness. Even the maidservant Nayana's cheerful bustle in the corridor becomes a relief. After chatting with Nayana, Jaya makes some lunch and again goes back to silence. Though Jaya has enjoyed freedom earlier, she now feels that she is not free in actuality, for Mohan has been following her with his looks. As Mohan calls Jaya loudly, Jaya feels the burden of his wanting, the burden of his clinging and she finds herself tied to him.

Jaya's experience in the Dadar flat is like going back to her childhood game of 'keeping house' she used to play in Saptagiri ajji's house along with her cousins. While Jaya is content in 'keeping house' in the Dadar flat, Mohan prowls restlessly about the house, unable to sit down in one place. The waiting is getting him down, he says. Jaya reflects that it is really hard for Mohan to wait, as he has never been used to it. She also notes a subtle difference between a man's approach to waiting and a woman's:

> He did not know what waiting was. He had always moved steadily from one moment to the next. But for women the waiting game starts early in childhood. *Wait until you get married. Wait until your husband comes. Wait until you go to your in-laws' home. Wait until you have kids.* (30)

There is waiting for the milk, for the servant and such others which are common to all women; Jaya had another waiting—a waiting for disaster, in addition to all these. She developed the belief that she cannot escape that disaster for long, that she must face it some day. When Mohan told her of the allegations of business malpractice against him, Jaya felt that her waiting for disaster came to its end. Unlike Jaya, Mohan had no belief in disasters. He tried to disown his responsibility and even justified his taking black money on the plea that no one can live just on salary. Mohan expected some words of consolation from Jaya, but she could say nothing. Nor could she explain Mohan's crime to him. Rather, she was compelled to share Mohan's sin.

> I racked my brains trying to think of an answer. And all that occurred to me was Sonia telling Raskolnikov—Confess your sins. Kneel down, kiss the earth and ask for forgiveness. But, I thought, he might well retort then—Kneel down yourself. Have you forgotten it is for you that I did this? For you and the children. . . . The children can plead ignorance and get off, but I will have to take on the burden of being a partner in the crime, an ally, an accessory before the fact.
>
> Kneel down yourself. . . . Yes, I will have to join him. The pair of us kneeling down and kissing the garbage-strewn, shit-

> pocked pavements of Bombay . . . hysteria gurgled in my throat. (31)

And this is because the society to which she belongs, likes to see her attached to her husband's sin. Jaya's silence is due to her inability to explain all this to Mohan who does not share Jaya's sensibility. Jaya has a perfect understanding of Mohan's thought-pattern. She admits that she was wrong in thinking that Mohan saw no ghosts. Mohan also has his ghosts which he now tries to exorcise by telling stories of his past. Mohan's remembrances of his childhood days included the activities of his mother, and Jaya gets the opportunity of reflecting on another silence, that of Mohan's mother. The unfortunate lady had to tolerate the whims and furies of her husband and Mohan explained her stoic silence as her strength. But Jaya "saw a despair so great that it would not voice itself . . . a struggle so bitter that silence was the only weapon." (36) The first part of the novel ends with another silence, that of Mohan's sister Vimala. She developed an ovarian tumour with metastases in the lungs, but could not tell anything to her in-laws who also did not bother about her health. When she was taken to hospital by her brother, she "sank into a coma and died a week later, her silence intact." (39) Thus the first part focuses on different types of silence which are studied and classified by Jaya as she analyses the nature and cause of her own silence.

Part II

The second part starts with the 'curious, convoluted history' of the Dadar flat which had been known as Makarand-mama's place and was then occupied by Jaya's elder brother who later gifted it to Jaya. The history of the flat gave the narrator a scope to describe persons somehow related to the flat—Makarand mama, his sister-in-law Vanitamami, her niece Kusum—and also the pictures hung on the wall of the flat by Makarand-mama. When Mohan and Jaya came to stay in the flat for the first time,

Mohan removed the pictures and the walls were coated with paints thrice. And yet, the rectangle marks of the photographs could be noted, as if "Makarand-mama was gently, unobtrusively, coming back to his old home." (46) Jaya nourishes the illusion for sometime that they had never moved away from the flat and that nothing has changed. Soon she returns to reality and accepts the fact that everything has changed following the rule of nature. And thus the narrator shifts easily from the past to the present. And while explaining the story of the children's tour, their friendship with Rupa and Ashok who insisted on taking the children with them, is also described. The maidservant Nayana's queries about the children made Jaya feels uneasy while the other maid Jeeja's silence gives Jaya an occasion to reflect on Jeeja's 'stoicism.' Several other characters are introduced and the novelist has the opportunity to focus on her feminist stand.

The second section of the second part starts with Jaya's recollection of Bombay when she first came there. A realistic description of the time and the place is rendered through Jaya's sensibility. Her past sensations are curiously merged with the present ones when she describes a procession, and the readers are almost caught unaware. Details of the couple's life in the flat, where they hardly talk except for the essentials of daily living, are exposed not only through Jaya's reflections but also through the intrusion of events outside (their next door neighbour's beating his wife, for example) on which both Jaya and Mohan comment, Mohan's being audible to Jaya who only talks to herself. Mohan is also affected by his memory and seeks to justify his effort for a transfer in the marketing division where he got scope for earning more. Earlier he gave the impression to Jaya that he got into trouble for taking action against a worker and not being happy with the stand of the authority, got transferred. But Mohan now discloses relentlessly that the decision had been taken much earlier when his father needed some extra money. With this revelation Jaya feels cheated and Mohan's deceitful nature as well as his immoral way of life is exposed. Jaya understands his character better than anybody else: it is his excessive attachment to materialism that explains his lying to himself, and to his wife and his inability to differentiate good from evil (moral good and evil).

There are other intrusions too, that of the young girl next door, for example, who wants to know if Jaya will take some vegetables from the vegetable seller. Though Jaya says that she needs none, the girl, Nilima, wants to spend time with Jaya when Mohan has left the flat. As Jaya faces the innocent queries of Nilima, she understands that her neighbours there are gossiping about their stay in the flat, leaving their aristocrat apartment in a posh area. After Nilima is taken away by her mother, Jaya, left to herself, gets relief. As Jaya sits at the table among books, Mohan may have the idea that Jaya is working for her fortnightly 'Seeta' story, but Jaya finds that 'Seeta' has suddenly exploded, that she cannot get even bits and pieces which could be put together. She is now in search of a new self as the old one that comes out from the pages of her diaries, appears to be quite a different person, an utter stranger. She admits that she did not disclose her heart in the pages of the diaries: "Its essential core had been left out. The agonized cries—'I can't cope, I can't manage, I can't go on'—had been neatly smothered." (70) This confession is the first step towards self-realization and Jaya tries her best to encounter her real self (or her real selves, as she opposes the idea of one integrated soul).

The sane housewife, as Jaya likes to call the lady who wrote the diaries, was split into several selves. One among them wrote down the sum that had been spent on ice cream the day they went to Juhu beach. This record reminds Jaya of some poor beggar-like children who were staring at Rahul and Rati licking ice cream cones, and moved in frantic movement to catch the remnant of Rahul's cone that he flung. That Jaya alias Suhasini suppressed the other self who had concern for the beggars becomes evident. But she has undergone a change recently. After her marriage her profession was to understand Mohan, but now she is not tuned to his moods. She went to their Churchgate house to receive the letters which were supposed to reach there. Mohan becomes impatient as he had to wait for her, for he is not habituated to that role. He expected some confidential letter from his colleague regarding the enquiry and is disappointed not to find any. Jaya cannot follow his thought any more because she no more thinks Mohan to be a sheltering tree. She appreciates Mohan's anxiety for her as she has been late, but also feels disappointed that Mohan, as usual, did no household chores to lessen her trouble. While cooking, Jaya remembers her earlier nature. Before her marriage, she would often express anger but was never taken seriously. But after marriage when she expressed her anger for the first time, Mohan took it very seriously. He looked at her as if her emotions made her ugly. Later she realized that according to him anger made a woman 'unwomanly,' and being terrified of his disapproval she learnt to control her anger. In his home, she discovered the differences between womanly and unwomanly behaviour. The women in his family were so well-trained that they always remained in the 'right' areas. Jaya almost regretted that she was never trained and she decided to pattern her life after those women. Now she realizes that she was foolish in doing so. She admits she had been ridiculously pleased after being praised for her perfect womanly manners. "The ghost scampered away with a grin at the sound of Mohan's voice"—This is how Deshpande shifts from the past to the present. Mohan wants to know if there is anything wrong with their phone in their Churchgate apartment, for he tried to phone Jaya when she went there, but could not. Jaya has to disclose that her younger brother Ravi rang up and that she would meet him near Dadar T.T. the next day.

The next section starts with Jaya's dream signifying her fear that she is late. Waking up, she recalls that her father also cared immensely about dreams and both of them would often discuss their dreams. She can now correlate the house seen in dream with a house in Saptagiri which was once shown to her by Mohan as the place where he, then a boy, first saw three convent-educated beautiful girls. Jaya understood that those women had given him his first vision of a different kind of life, a life that had none of the poverty, the shabbiness and ugliness, the rigid rules and rituals he had known till then. Mohan also told her that Jaya seemed to him to be one of those three girls when he saw her for the first time. Jaya then thanked his father for sending her to convent school. All these past thoughts help Jaya to reflect on 'education and culture' loosely used by persons who hardly have any real ideas about these. Deshpande displays her unique narrative skill in keeping side by side the past and the present through Jaya's critical analysis of her sexual experiences. The second part of the novel ends with Jaya's decision that she must remove Mohan's wrong notion that she is still continuing the column of 'Seeta.'

Part III

The third part starts with a conversation between Ravi and Jaya who is trying her best to give an impression that everything is going on well with her family lest there be any suspicion in Ravi's mind with regard to Mohan's career. Ravi's presence wells up her childhood memories affecting her emotions. But when he says that their mother complained about her rare visits to Ambegaon to see her mother, uncle and aunt, Jaya is angry as she remembers the old story of Chandumama's financing her college dues after her father's death. She has always tried to ignore the fact but at the same time cannot altogether neglect the three old persons. She also expresses her anger when Ravi makes fun with the feminine desire of motherhood while referring to Vanitamami. Ignoring her reprimand Ravi goes on describing other things and both were linked by common memory. Lastly,

Jaya takes the responsibility of contacting the nurse, known to them, for Vanitamami's treatment and of bringing her mother and Vanitamami to her place in Bombay. Ravi expresses his inability to take them to his home as his wife Asha has gone to her father's place. Ravi also asks Jaya to take initiative in settling up their conjugal quarrel. It is also revealed that Ravi heard about Mohan's troubles in office and even proposes Jaya to lend a helping hand through a political leader. Jaya, however, shows her common sense through her denial of any trouble. The strained relationship of Ravi and Asha reminds her naturally of the past days when Asha was pampered for her wealth and beauty.

With Deshpande the stream-of-consciousness technique is no more a strenuous effort on the part of the reader to follow the track of the protagonist's thought process. The process is spontaneous and hence quite natural. Jaya's sojourn in the past is thus naturally disturbed by Mohan's inquiry about Ravi's intention. Jaya tells him that Ravi was inquiring about the trouble in Mohan's office and Mohan is naturally upset that the scam has been disclosed. Jaya sees Mohan unmasked now, as he overtakes her with his repeated queries about what exactly Ravi has known. And Mohan's concern leaves him almost a fanatic and he charges Jaya with total unconcern in his problem. He even brings the accusation that Jaya's only concern has always been the comfort supplied by Mohan, though she hardly bothers about Mohan's problems in the office. Mohan's accusation directly takes her to the past days, leaving her in an angry confusion. Jaya feels that Mohan has armed himself with an anger underneath which there is genuine hostility. He accuses her of not taking care about the children, of isolating herself from the family and her own feeble defences fail before this fierce onslaught. She feels as if she has been struck dumb, pinned to her own place by his anger which is like a monstrously huge spear going through her and yet leaving her fully conscious. He further says that all women are like this and thereon Jaya interrupts with her question if he knows what type of woman she is. As Mohan goes on describing in a changed tone that he has not failed to note her change after they came to the Dadar flat, Jaya notes a child-like confusion in his face and just cannot check her hysteric laughter. Mohan stares at her in horror and then leaves home.

The remaining portion of the third part of the novel deals with Jaya in the lonely flat. Stupefied by Mohan's sudden departure and by the aftermath of his accusation, Jaya is now free to recall other incidents in the past that left her almost equally stupefied. Her father's sudden death on the day of her first S.S.C. examination and the effect of that sudden blow on her are recollected as vivid images. And then there are poetic renderings of her relationship with Kamat and the blow of his sudden death. As Jaya says, memory is selective and through her words the writer justifies herself for selecting only the relevant parts from Jaya's memory. It is however not just Jaya's memory that weaves the thread of the narrative. Both memory and the present happenings are woven together to produce the wonderful structure. Thus Jaya is not left unnoticed after she is deserted by Mohan. Her neighbour, the young widow Mukta, and Mukta's daughter Nilima, come to Jaya as members of the present world and Jaya is forced to remain in the present time. Her memories are blended with her conversations to form the texture of the novel that centres on her decision to emerge as a writer who is true to herself and is afraid of nothing, not even of losing her shelter. She is required to reassess her relationship with all those whom she has known, even those who are already dead, for she realizes that it is only with the dead that one can have a perfect relationship. The third part of the novel concludes with her recognition that her whole being had responded to Kamat's call which she rejected and later when she went to him he was dead and that night she used Mohan's body only to release her emotions provoked by Kamat.

Part IV

The fourth part of the novel shows no change in the setting. Jaya is still alone in her Dadar flat as Mohan has not come yet. But she has little time now for idle brooding. She goes to hospital to arrange treatment for Rajaram, the step-son of the maid Jeeja. Rajaram, a drunkard, was stabbed by some 'goondas' who drank with his money and when all was spent made Rajaram ask for more drink without money and being refused, stabbed him. Jaya visits the doctor on duty and luckily he happens to be her elder brother's friend, Dr. Vyas. He assures that he will do whatever is needed and Jaya goes to their Churchgate apartment. Perhaps she has expected Mohan to be there and gets a bit disappointed when she finds the house empty. A matter of concern has been waiting for her. Servants from the neighbouring household inform her that their phone was ringing continuously, and when it took some interval it started again. No sooner do the servants inform her than the phone starts ringing again. At first Jaya becomes so nervous that she cannot even move. She feels that something must have been ominous about the ring. Then she thinks that it might be Mohan's. But when she takes the receiver she is horrified to hear the voice of her friend Rupa who took Jaya's children with her on a family tour. And it is indeed a matter of grave concern that Jaya's son Rahul has gone away without telling them anything. As Jaya puts down the receiver, it sticks to her clammy palm. Her body has become dripping wet. The room being stifling hot, she switches on the fan and the sudden burst of air makes her shiver. Not knowing what to do, she goes to the window and gives it a push. As it does not open, she bangs it hard with her fist and it flows open. And a crow lands on the window as it opens and Jaya cannot drive it off. It continues to croak and then abruptly flies off, leaving Jaya in a horrifying state. And then the phone rings again and this time it is from Mohan's brother Vasant who informs that Rahul is with him. Jaya talks to Rahul on phone and asks him to go to Dadar flat.

With so many confusing matters in her brain, Jaya starts for the Dadar flat and waits under a bus shade when it is raining so heavily. She notices two young men and a girl in objectionable postures and cannot resist shouting at them. But they ignore her and she runs out of the bus shelter to escape the scene. She reaches the flat somehow, in an unconscious state suffering from high fever, as it is learnt from Mukta and Nilima. As Jaya comes to her senses and feels little better, she finds Mukta accompanying her. While answering Mukta's query, Jaya confesses that perhaps Mohan has left her. Thereon Mukta asks her if it is for Kamat. Surprised, Jaya tells her that Kamat has nothing to do in their case. Mukta then accuses Jaya of leaving dying Kamat alone in his room. Jaya had no idea that she was being closely observed by Mukta. She also learns of Mukta's strong emotions for Kamat who has helped her to stand on her own. A new vista is opened up before her eyes. Her newly acquired knowledge about Kamat and Mukta helps her to recognize her own self too. "The loneliness of a man facing his death—is there anything like it in this world? His pain filled this room and we could both of us feel it, Mukta and I. The fellowship of pain seemed to bind us together; we were like two patients in a hospital, suffering from the same disease, lying on two adjacent beds." (186)

At the end of the novel Rahul returns home, accompanied by Vasant, and there is also Mohan's telegram saying 'all well.' These outward facts are perfectly blended with the dimensional depth of Jaya's consciousness. In fact, almost all the activities except the departure of Mohan and Rahul and the accident of Rajaram, take place in Jaya's mind and there is hardly any forward movement. Flashbacks are extensively used to trace the evolution of Jaya's consciousness and to show how she emerges as a writer who is true to herself. The process of her self-realization being complete, she goes back to the papers on which she has been scribbling. She reflects on her frightened and desperate self which is now subdued by her fearless spirit. She feels that the panic is gone. Earlier she thought that she must survive only as Mohan's wife and that the bits of her self that refused to be Mohan's wife must be cut off. Now she understands that that kind of fragmentation is not possible. She reçalls Daniel Defoe's words that fiction is 'a sort of lying that makes a great hole in the heart at which by degrees a habit of lying enters in.' Jaya likes little bits of fiction but cannot think of living with a hole in heart. She now rejects the image of two bullocks yoked together, for this does not give a real picture. In order to plug that hole in heart she has to erase the silence in between them. Deshpande's unique narrative skill blends the interior monologue with the ebb and flow of outward incidents including dialogue among several characters. The novel's strength lies in its capacity to capture the reader's attention through a spell of narration.

NOTES

1. Jaya is able to see her and her family in a detached way:

> A picture of the four of us at a meal came to me in the same way, like a glossy, coloured advertising visual. We smiled, we laughed; I, the mother, served them with 'love and care'; Mohan, the head of the family, smiled indulgently, and the children were lively and playful. A visual—yes it had to be only that; for I could not find the words to match the picture. (4)

2. Jaya says, "I remember now how often I had sighed for a catastrophe, a disaster, no, not a personal one, but anything to shake us out of our dull grooves." (4) This hankering after outward disaster reveals that Jaya was suffering from monotony and boredom from which she sought a relief. If she could express herself in her writings, she might not have felt bored.
3. Mohan is actually lying to herself. He is so much entangled by the comforts and power of the materialistic world that his conscience

is suppressed. He is in the condition of what Sartre calls 'bad faith.' Sartre has it, "To be sure, the one who practises bad faith is hiding a displeasing truth or presenting as truth a pleasing untruth. Bad faith then has in appearance the structure of falsehood. Only what changes everything is the fact that in bad faith it is from myself that I am hiding the truth." (*Being and Nothingness*, trans. Hazel E. Barnes, p. 49)

4. Shashi Deshpande touches the theme of madwoman in the attic, a theme popularized by the feminists. In the male-controlled society, women were forced to remain silent and they were hardly given any scope to protest. Their suppressed emotions would often leave them insane. The character of Bertha Mason in Charlotte Bronte's *Jane Eyre* has been seriously studied by the feminists all over the world. Kusum's madness in *That Long Silence* reminds one of Bertha and other madwomen in literature.

Feminism and *That Long Silence*

A demand for equal status for women in the male-dominated society was heard in nineteenth century Europe and gradually this demand developed into a struggle for women's rights in the early twentieth century. In North America, Feminism emerged as one of the most powerful social, cultural and political movements. Mary Wollstonecraft's *A Vindication of the Rights of Woman (*1792) launched a powerful attack on the second class status of women, an attack that was in the line of her continuous publications on women's issues such as *Thoughts on the Education of Daughters* (1787) and *The Wrongs of Woman: or Maria* (published posthumously). John Stuart Mill's *The Subjection of Women* (1869) and Margaret Fuller's *Women in the Nineteenth Century* (1845), among others, were radical responses to the conservative opinion. Virginia Woolf's *A Room of One's Own* (1929) and numerous other essays paved the way for feminist literary criticism. A much more radical approach was launched by Simone de Beauvoir's *The Second Sex* (1949). Simon de Beauvoir suffered from a terrible male envy for the female physiology, and complained against the physiological problems of womanhood. She opposed the cultural identification of women as merely the negative object, or 'Other' to man. Feminist literary criticism as a self-conscious approach was, however, as late as 1960s to be visible. Two important modern feminist approaches to literary criticism of the time were Mary Ellman's *Thinking about Women* and Kate Millett's *Sexual Politics,* both published in1968. Mary Ellman protested against the derogatory stereotypes of women in literary works by men, and also against the subversive points of view in some women's writings. Millett pointed at the manipulation of power by the male and the dominance of men in every sector of society. Feminist literary criticism flourished after that with an urgency and excitement that can hardly be seen with any literary movement.

Broadly speaking, feminist criticism launches its attack on patriarchal ideology, on the prevailing concepts of gender and on the marginalized roles allotted to women in the male-governed society. This patriarchal ideology teaches women to internalize this concept in the process of their socialization. Diverse post-structuralist theories as well as psychoanalytic and Marxist approaches have also been included in feminist literary criticism. That the differences in race, class, nationality and historical situation stand on the way of uniform female identities is highlighted by these critics. Barbara Johnson's *A World of Difference* (1987), Rita Felski's *Beyond Feminist Aesthetics: Feminist Literature and Social Change* (1989), *The Norton Anthology of Literature by Women* edited by Sandra Gilbert and Susan Gubar, Toril Moi's *Sexual/Textual Politics: Feminist Literary Theory* (1985) are a few examples from the vast body of Feminist theoretical and critical writings. As a movement, however, feminism is marked by contradictions; but those who remain outside the movement, feminism appears to be shaped by a unified monolithic vision. The female novelists in the last two decades of the twentieth century have been greatly influenced by these feminist writings and they appear to be totally conscious of the feminist trends of the time, focusing on the genuine issues that a woman has to confront in her family and in the society. Margaret Laurence's *The Diviners,* Margaret Atwood's *Bodily Harm,* Mary McCarthy's *The Groves of Academme,* Anita Desai's *Fire on the Mountain* are instances of modern novels by the women writers who introduced feminist issues that have been raised by the writers for several decades.

Shashi Deshpande is fully aware of those disturbing issues, but she deals with those issues in a different way. She projects women in a man-woman situation, rather than in an exclusive man's world. She is also aware of the fact that in spite of countless instances of atrocities committed against the Indian women at various stages, the myths have always treated them with honour and this treatment was not necessarily a way of deceiving the women folk. Moreover, unlike say, Simon de Beauvoir, Shashi has not looked upon female physiology as a burden. Among the physiological problems of the women, it is pregnancy alone that she takes up with concern; for, the period of pregnancy demands great caution and extra care which are hardly provided to the women in India. She does not forget to accept pregnancy as a privilege for the women. She says in an interview,

> The women in my books are people who come to realize what it is to be a woman in the process of their own lives and the situations they face not through books and theories. I think feminism is an entirely personalized perception. It is when you start questioning preconceived notions about your roles. I don't think there is anything 'inherent' in a woman apart from the fact that she can conceive. All other things are equally important for them as they are for the men.[1]

Deshpande makes her stand as a feminist clear in the above statement. Though she is fully aware of the existing trends of feminist criticism, she hardly copies them. Instead, she criticizes the preconceived notions whenever she feels an urge to do so. Otherwise she accepts the normal condition of the society where both men and women have contributed to the plight of women.

Among the preconceived notions that are criticized in the novel, the elimination of the girl child from the 'family tree' is perhaps the most important. Once Jaya's Ramu Kaka excitedly showed her the family tree prepared by him. He was proud to proclaim that he had gone back nearly two hundred years to trace the line of their ancestors. But Jaya was shocked to find her name missing. The conversation between Jaya and Ramu Kaka may be quoted to show Jaya's shock and her ignorance as her father had hardly given her any scope to think about her difference from the male members (her brothers, for example,) in the family.

> "I've been able to go back for nearly two hundred years. There are a few gaps, of course, but I'll fill them up eventually. Look, Jaya, this is our branch. This is our grandfather—your great grandfather—and here's father, and then us—Laxman, Vasu and me. And here are the boys—Shridhar, Jannu, Dinkar, Ravi. . . ."
>
> "But Ramukaka," I'd exclaimed, "I'm not here!"
>
> "You!" He had looked up, irritated by the interruption, impatient at my stupidity. "How can you be here? You don't belong to this family! You're married, you're now part of Mohan's family. You have no place here."
>
> At this point, as I had been narrating this story to Mohan, Mohan had smiled. "Of course, your Ramukaka is right. You belong to my family now."
>
> Okay, I'd wanted to ask Ramukaka, if I don't belong to this family, what about the *Kakis* and Ai? They married into this family, didn't they, why are they not here? And what about *ajji*, who single-handedly kept the family together, why isn't she here?
>
> But I had said nothing—neither to Ramukaka, nor to Mohan. *Ajji* should be pleased with me. I had learnt it at last—no questions, no retorts. Only silence. (142-43)

The fact that the family tree does not include any woman reveals the utter lack of importance for women in the Indian social set up. Jaya is also aware that the Indian women have been treated not only with negligence, but also with physical torture. Manda's description of her mother's suffering leads Jaya to reflect on the condition of the poor Indian women:

> Where was it I had read an account of how baby girls were done to death a century or so back? They were, I had read in horror, buried alive, crushed to death in the room they were born in; and immedi-

> ately after that, a fire was lit on the spot—to purify the place, they said. Perhaps it was to ensure death. (53)

Jaya's anger and despair over the inhuman treatment inflicted on the women in Indian society is artistically rendered in the novel.

Shashi Deshpande analyses the problems faced by the Indian women belonging to different strata of life. Her approach to the problems of women is serious as she is a serious writer, but she does not like to be treated as a so-called feminist. She says,

> It is a curious fact that serious writing by women is invariably regarded as feminist writing—A woman who writes of women's experiences often brings in some aspects of those experiences that have angered her, roused her strong feelings. I don't see why this has to be labelled feminist fiction. A (male) critic once said about a novel of mine, "She can be quite brilliant when she is not raising her banners of protest." What banners of protest, was my thought. Any woman who writes fiction shows the world as it looks to her protagonist: if the protagonist is a woman, she shows the world as it looks to a woman—to apply the tag of feminist is one way, I have realized, of dismissing the serious concerns of the novel by labelling them, by calling the work propagandist.[2]

She further says,

> When a man writes of the particular problems a man is facing, he is writing male propaganda. Nobody says that, why is it said only about women writers?[3]

Deshpande's novels are yet discussed by some critics as feminist novels. But it will be a great mistake to assert that she is supporting the western individualistic feminism. Rather, she comes close to Chaman Nahal's definition of feminism. Chaman Nahal says,

> I define feminism as a mode of existence in which the woman is free of the dependence syndrome. There is a dependence syndrome: whether it is the husband or the father or the community or whether it is a religious group, ethnic group, when women free

> themselves of the dependence syndrome and lead a normal life, my idea of feminism materializes.[4]

The protagonists in Deshpande's novels do not depend on any religious or ethnic group. And when they find 'dependence syndrome' in themselves, they try to free themselves; unlike Ibsen's Nora, however, they may remain at home with their male counterparts but they change themselves internally, learning how to assert individuality. They often develop a world-view that enables them to see themselves in terms of relationships and of human values.[5] The women protagonists in Deshpande's novels go beyond what Elaine Showalter calls the 'Female Phase.'[6]

The very title of the novel *That Long Silence* brings Shashi Deshpande close to the feminist thinkers. The title is derived from a speech given by the American actress Elizabeth Robins to W.W.S.L. in 1907. Robins said, "If I were a man and cared to know the world I lived in, I almost think it would make me a shade uneasy, the weight of that long silence." This 'long silence' was however taken up as their subject by a good number of women writers, but most of them lapsed into sentimental romances as they almost failed to delve deep into the superficial matters. In contrast with her predecessors who either dwelt on superficial matters or succumbed to the feminist ideology, Deshpande studies facts and projects the 'silence' of all sorts of women facing different types of problems.

The choice of a writer as the protagonist of her novel helped Deshpande to render credibility to her writing. Jaya, the protagonist of the novel, has been portraying characters who belong to the make-believe world, and she is aware that she avoids reality. She remembers how her first attempt to reveal reality was interpreted by her husband as an act of profanation (Mohan accused her of blaming her husband through her story), and since then her career has been jeopardized. She starts writing under an assumed name, but her stories are rejected. She remembers the comment of her neighbour Kamat that her stories are lacking in strong emotions and that a woman's story is supposed to express anger. Jaya almost echoed her husband when she argued, "A woman can never be angry. She can only be neurotic, hysterical, frustrated." (147) As a perceptive critic, Kamat gave her a warning: "Beware of this 'women are the victims' theory of yours. It'll drag you down into a soft, squishy bog of self-pity. Take yourself seriously, woman. Don't skulk behind a false name." (148) Through Kamat's accusations, Deshpande criticizes those women writers (the Indian women writers, in particular) who continue to idealize the women, ignoring reality.

Kamat's suggestion did not however have any immediate effect on Jaya. Instead of showing anger in her stories she started writing light humorous pieces on the travails of middle-class housewives in a column entitled 'SEETA.' This column received good responses from all sides including Mohan, and Jaya felt 'secured' as she could maintain peace in the family. Dissecting her creative self, Jaya acknowledges,

> She [Seeta] had been the means through which I had shut the door, firmly on all those other women who had invaded my being, screaming for attention; women I had known I could not write about, because they might—it was just possible—resemble Mohan's mother or aunt or my mother or aunt. (149)

A writer's fear to face the reality could hardly be better described. Jaya finally wins over her fear during her stay in the Dadar flat and acquires necessary courage to overlook Mohan's reactions. Through the process of Jaya's self-realization and her memories, all the characters of real life that she had earlier avoided, appear and Deshpande utilizes the opportunity of introducing real women encountering real problems of life.

A brief discussion of how the women characters in *That Long Silence* are focused will reveal Deshpande's acute concern for the position of women in the male-governed society, a concern that explains her affinity with the feminists. Take Kusum's story first. She was the niece of Jaya's aunt (Vanitamami) who, being childless, took up Kusum as her own daughter. Kusum did not have beauty, charm and wealth and thus became an easy prey to male antagonism. She had no intelligence either and Jaya too developed a dislike towards her, a dislike that was later tempered to an indifferent contempt. Jaya explains what in particular irritated her:

> Even as a gaunt, unattractive girl, Kusum had emphasized her femaleness. She had aped a grown woman, swinging her skinny hips from side to side in a grotesque parody of a woman's walk. She had begun wearing a sari when she was barely thirteen, pulling the end of it scrupulously round her shoulders, covering herself fully, as if to hide her barely perceptible breasts from possibly lecherous males. Whenever Dada was about, she would sidle past him with a kind of exaggerated modesty that had both enraged me and made me want to laugh. (21)

That insignificant Kusum was married and gave birth to three children all of whom were girls. Desperate to have a male child of her own, Kusum developed insanity and was rejected by her husband. At that stage Jaya took the initiative, arranging for Kusum's treatment and her stay in the Dadar flat, much to Mohan's opposition.[7] Jaya resisted when Mohan tried to stop her from helping Kusum, and this was Jaya's first straight fight against Mohan. Kusum could not yet be saved. She insisted on going back to her 'home' where everybody despised her. When Jaya rudely told her that her children did not need her, Kusum replied that she needed them. Jaya had no answer to that and Kusum was gone. After a few days she threw herself in a well and died. Jaya's reflections on Kusum render her as the 'Other' or the 'Double' of Jaya and the description receives a new dimension:

> I could feel her anguish, her fears, her despair. They seeped into me drop by drop, until I felt myself burdened with them. The day I heard she was sick, I felt relief. It was like hearing of someone's death. Your own life, your living, becomes a vital truth you're

> suddenly conscious of. And so with Kusum's madness I became aware of my own blessed sanity. Thank God, Kusum, you're nuts, I had thought; because you're that, I know I'm balanced, normal and sane.
>
> Suddenly it occurs to me—as long as Kusum was there, I had known clearly who I was. I was not Kusum. Now, with Kusum dead. . .? (24)

The above passage reminds one of the feminist interpretations of Charlotte Bronte's *Jane Eyre.* Bertha Mason, the mad woman in the attic, is rendered as Jane's double. The above passage renders Kusum as Jaya's Double almost in a similar way.[8]

While Kusum is an embodiment of negative qualities, some other women characters in the novel are denied proper attention and opportunities, and suffer from insecurity. Childless Vanitamami is one such character who suffers from insecurity in a male-dominated society where the household is dominated and ruled by the elderly mother-in-law, and the daughters-in-law have no way but to digest humiliations. It is her sense of insecurity that prompted Vanitamami to give an advice to Jaya in regard to her attitude to her husband. She tells that a husband is a sheltering tree for ever and the wife should ignore even if he keeps a mistress. Jaya also could not understand why of all her sister's brood, Vanitamami had taken to the feeble, spiritless Kusum. She concludes later that perhaps Vanitamami had never known what it was to choose. Since her mother-in-law's death, Vanitamami had changed completely. She became aggressive, letting loose her pent-up rage. Jaya's mother, who had been staying in her brother's home, dominating his family for last twenty years, could not anymore cope with the metamorphosed Vanitamami and was desperately looking out for a place she could retreat to. Deshpande's hold on psychology is thus blended with her feminist stand.

With Mohan's mother and sister, the surrounding was more cruel and suffocating.[9] Even Mohan is unaware of the facts about his mother's death which were told to Jaya by Mohan's sister Vimala. Vimala says that her mother always remained pregnant and she did not want the last child. Being desperate, she went to a midwife to get her aborted, and died a painful death. Vimala's description of her mother's silent suffering is horrifying:

> I didn't bother until I heard her screams. I didn't even imagine it was her screaming at first, it wasn't like her voice at all, it was a thin, ugly voice that scared me to death. And then, as I watched, she began hitting herself on the face. Her hands were all floury, and wet too, and her face soon became white and flowery. Soon there were red patches as she went on and on hurting herself. I tried to stop her; I tried to stop her screams, I tried to hold her hands, but I could do nothing. Her hands were like . . . steel. At last her hands slowed down and I could hold them. She began to cry. I tried to make her lie down, I tried to make her drink some water, but she just went on saying, "I can't, I can't." She lay near the fire moaning. Her body had become like a . . ..like a stuffed doll's. . . . At last she stopped crying and lay still, breathing heavily. . . . A week later she died. (38)

Mohan's father was a drunkard and he would come home late every night compelling her wife to wait with hot meal to serve him. He wanted his rice fresh and hot, from a vessel that was untouched. Mohan described how one day he threw his rice plate at the wall as there was no fresh chutney that day. The poor wife picked up the plate and cleansed the floor silently and then went to prepare chutney, after lighting the fire and blowing it. When the baby woke up and began to cry, she hushed it and gave it her breast. When the baby finally drifted off to sleep, she sat in front of the fire, silent and motionless. Describing the incident, Mohan commented that women those days were tough. Jaya's view was different. She said, "He saw strength in the woman sitting silently in front of the fire, but I saw despair. I saw a despair so great that it would not voice itself. I saw a struggle so bitter that silence was the only weapon. Silence and surrender." (36)This is a direct attack on the patriarchal system and for such attacks Deshpande is called a feminist, though her approach is different from that of some well-known feminists of the western world.

Besides Mohan's mother, there is Mohan's sister Vimala who also died in silence. She was suffering from an ovarian tumour with metastases in the lungs, but she did not tell anyone about her illness. Why she preferred silence is clear from the words of her mother-in-law which are quoted by Jaya without further comment:

> 'All that bleeding,' they had whispered after death, the women in her husband's home. When Mohan and I had visited her—our normal routine visit during our annual stay in Saptagiri—her mother-in-law had shrugged heavily and said, 'God knows what is wrong with her. She has lying there on her bed for over a month now. Yes, take her away if you want to. I never heard of women going to hospitals and doctors for such a thing. As if other women don't have heavy periods! What a fuss! But these women who've never had children are like that.' (39)

The above passage displaying a woman's callousness, inhumanity and rudeness causing another woman's death highlights the distinctness of Deshpande's attitude. She does not put the blame only on the men for their antagonistic attitude; the women are equally blamed. These women are so moulded by the existing pattern of the society that they are unable to think freely. Jaya's ajji and other ajji (her paternal and maternal grandmother), Mukta's mother and such other women, who deny human rights to other women and exercise their power on those women, belong to this group.

Among the working class women, the picture is hardly better. Though they earn money doing odd jobs all over the day, they are prey to all sorts of maltreatment, and are burdened with repeated pregnancy against their will. Nayana and Tara are such typical Indian women who cling to their husbands despite their various tortures simply because they owe their 'kumkum,' the mark of married women, to them. The elderly woman Jeeja is markedly distinct among the lot. Jaya refers to Jeeja's 'reticence' or 'stoicism,' and she even envies Jeeja's 'single mindedness.' As she says, "She knew what her purpose in life was—it was to go on living. Enduring was part of it and so she endured all that she had to." (51)

When she started working for Jaya, she asked her mistress not to give her husband any of her pay, giving hints thereby what her life was like. Jaya calls her a realist, not loyal, because she knew that she was earning more money than other servants only because of her reliability, and that she badly needed money. A 'pure professional' like Jeeja is indeed rare among her class. But her views of life are hardly different from others. Jaya is surprised to see no anger behind her silence. When asked by Jaya, she expressed her feelings which reveal her sympathetic understanding of others including her husband who appears to be the cause of her suffering. Jeeja told that her husband was not from the beginning a drunkard. Only after he lost his job at the time of a strike that he started drinking. Moreover, she was denied the blessing of having any issue and so she cannot blame her husband for marrying again. Jeeja even had the broadness of mind to look after the children of his husband's second wife after her death. When after her husband's death Jeeja found her son stepping into his father's shoes, she took it up as her responsibility to look after the family of the son. The daughter-in-law Tara has three children and she is lacking in Jeeja's toughness and resilience. She has been trailing Jeeja from door to door, doing all the odd jobs. And whenever she moans her fate wishing her husband's death, Jeeja reminds her that "he keeps the 'kumkum' on your forehead. What is a woman without that?" (53)

While projecting this picture of exploitation of woman by the society which is governed by age-old ideas created by men for their comfort, Deshpande does not forget to make her protagonist reflect on exploitations of the poor by the rich. Jaya says, "It was Jeeja and her like I needed; it was these women who saved me from the hell of drudgery. Any little freedom I had depended on them." (52) Thus Deshpande is above all a humanist who centres on the problems faced by the Indian women and offers a realist's view of life, one that is not limited by any dogma.

Deshpande is also aware of the pernicious effect of the catchy slogans of Women's Lib on the affluent families who have no faith in traditional values. To illustrate her point she incorporates the incident of a jeans-clad beautiful and educated girl accompanied by two young men. "The girl had a face of remarkable beauty and delicacy. A slim body clad in jeans. On the whole, a beauty that was appalling in its perfection . . . the girl snatched at a cigarette one of the men was smoking. He feigned unwillingness then, yielding, put it between her parted, exquisitely tender lips. She took a deep drag, eyes closed in ecstasy, and the two men watched her with the detached interest of scientists observing the results of an experiment. One of them . . . was openly fondling the girl's small breasts. She opened her eyes and the men laughed. She laughed too—a thin, ugly laugh that went on and on. The cigarette was roughly pulled away from her lips by the man. She tried to grab it. The man moved away. She got up, swayed, tottered and leaned against the other man." (174) Jaya is horrified at the spectacle. Unable to remain a mute witness to this annihilation of womanhood, she protests, but only in vain. And then she prefers to walk away in drenching rain, leaving the bus-stop shelter. The incident sends the message: if by the name of Women's Freedom the young women make themselves easy prey to man's lust, it would be a horrible and idiotic imitation of the obscene, lustful way of life and not freedom.

That Long Silence is unique not as much for its treatment of women in general, as for its revelation of the interior world of a woman writer, its protagonist, Jaya. The conflict between Jaya the writer and Jaya the housewife is exposed with a clarity that is indeed rare. Thanks to her acute self-consciousness and her capacity of self-dissection, Jaya knows why she maintains silence. For seventeen long years she has tried to mould her in a pattern that would satisfy Mohan as well as others in the society. This new self that was born after her marriage is referred to as Suhasini, the name given to her by Mohan. Though no one called her by the new name, she is 'officially' known as Suhasini after her marriage and has accepted the role of Suhasini, that is, the role of a married lady. Kamat laughed when he heard of this new name, but Jaya continued to remain Suhasini, eliminating her other self that has always been true to herself. Once after her marriage she wrote a story about the relationship of a woman and a man who cannot approach his wife without his body. When the story was published Mohan took it to be an insult to him, for, as he explained to Jaya, the story was taken by people as the story of Mohan, and he was humiliated.[10] Mohan behaved in such a way that Jaya was compelled to stop writing. Jaya says, "Looking at his stricken face, I had been convinced, I had done him wrong. And I had stopped writing after that." (144) She did not know how to explain her point of view to one who had never shared her feelings. In short, she was afraid to face the atrocities that were likely to be generated by her writings.

Moreover, she did not want to confront insecurity; almost in the manner of Vanitamami she accepted Mohan as the sheltering tree. That is why she did not bother to know if Mohan was following some unethical ways for earning money. Rather she kept her aloof from reality and took shelter in a make-believe world, writing for a Woman's Magazine under the pseudo name of Seeta. But she cannot stay long in that secure world which she had taken for granted. Mohan is suspected to be involved in a shady deal and an enquiry into the charge of corruption brought against Mohan is anticipated. On the advice of his colleague who is also anticipating similar enquiry, Mohan comes to stay in the Dadar flat and as it is expected, Jaya comes with him. The children, Rahul and Rati, being away on a long tour with their family friends, Mohan feels comfortable as he need not explain to them why he has shifted. Regarding Jaya he takes it for granted that he owes no explanation to her, that she is compelled to follow her husband into 'exile,' following the footsteps of the mythical figures such as Sita and Draupadi. In the silence of the Dadar flat, when Jaya delves deep into her mind scrutinizing her role as a wife and a mother and also as a contributor in a Woman's Magazine, she is rudely shocked by the jolt received from Mohan. Unable to gauge Jaya's silence, Mohan tells her, "I did it for you and for the children." Mohan accused Jaya that she had extracted comfort from him, without feeling for him and now that they were compelled to leave their furnished flat and came to Dadar, she has become unhappy. Mohan angrily says that if he had done any wrong it was for the comfort of Jaya and the children, and thus Jaya also becomes a party to the crime. Thanks to this blow from Mohan, Jaya is led to a more critical self-analysis and exposes her deceitful role as a writer.

When Jaya started writing for the column of Seeta, she abstained from telling the truth. She ceased to think of herself as an individual, and posed to be happy with the role of a wife and a mother. Now she confesses that the characters she introduced through the column of Seeta shut the door firmly on all those women who had invaded her being, screaming for attention. She could not write about those women, because they might resemble Mohan's mother or aunt or her own mother or aunt. Through this confessional statement by Jaya, Deshpande attacks the mode of writing of some women writers who attain cheap popularity with their works that have little to do with reality. Jaya's recollection of Kamat's contemptuous view of her writing also adds to the same effect. Kamat said to Jaya, "I can never imagine you writing this. This you, I mean. I can see the woman who writes this. She's plump, good humoured, pea brained, but shrewd, devious, skimming over life." (149) Kamat also told Jaya to take her seriously and not to write behind a false name. When Jaya is forced to see the reality after receiving the jolt from Mohan, she remembers that Kamat told her that she had been scared of writing. She confesses that she was actually scared of writing the facts of life:

> Middle class. Bourgeoise. Upper-caste. Distanced from real life. Scared of writing. Scared of failing. Oh God, I had thought, I can't take any more. Even a worm has a hole it can crawl into. I had mine—as Mohan's wife, as Rahul's and Rati's mother.
>
> And so I had crawled back into my hole. I had felt safe there. Comfortable. Unassailable. And so I had stopped writing. It hadn't been Mohan's fault at all. And it had been just a coincidence, though it had helped, that just then Mohan had propelled me into that other kind of writing. 'I encouraged you,' he had said to me. He was right. But I went on with my chest-beating fit of penitence; Mohan had not forced me to do that kind of writing. I'd gone into it myself. With my eyes wide open. (148)

Here is a wonderful experiment with the revelation of a writer's conflict, a woman writer who wrote imaginary matters about women under the mythical name 'Seeta,' and who now seriously wants to emerge out of her previous stand. Detached from her children and her usual way of life in the luxurious apartment, Jaya asks her inner self whether the kind of life she has been living should at all be accepted. "What do you want? . . . Just to live. To know that at the end of the day my family and I are under a roof, safe, enclosed, in a secure world. If it is dark outside, what does it matter? I can close the door and windows, switch on the lights and the darkness will recede." (181-82) This awareness is something greater than the one introduced by a typical feminist. The woman protagonist emerges out of her selfish existence to embrace the outer reality. Jaya goes to hospital to contact a doctor for the treatment of Rajaram, as she now believes that life should bear a meaning for every individual. To quote Adele King in this context,

> In a self-referential parody, Deshpande makes Jaya a writer of woman's magazine fiction. In Jaya's stories they lived happily ever after although she knows the falsity of the view of life. Also, the mixture of surrealism and fantasy in some of the experiences the writer undergoes is an important aspect of the making and unmaking of fictions in *That Long Silence.*[11]

The novel may thus be discussed as a critique of so-called women's writing that fails to depict the real problems faced by the women in real life.

Deshpande does not like to be called a feminist for she does not like to see her surrounding from a biased point of view. That is why her novel includes male characters (Kamat and Jaya's father in *That Long Silence*) that make no difference between man and woman, and also female characters (Jaya's ajji, her mother) that are responsible for the sufferings of other women. Moreover, she likes her protagonist to be, above all, a humanist who is able to understand others' point of view. Thus Jaya understands very well that when Mohan projects him as a broad-minded man who always fulfilled Jaya's wish, it is of no use to shout at him, to tell him that he did not approve of the job she wanted to take, the baby she had wanted to adopt, the anti-price campaign she had liked to join. She feels that Mohan had nothing to with these; but it was she whose will was not perfect. "Perhaps I had not really cared enough about these things myself." (120)

After this realization she also admits to herself that she has moulded her to fit in with Mohan's dream, as she could not, till then, form her own dream of life. Jaya also feels that Mohan has known that Suhasini is dead, and he has to encounter 'Jaya' from now on. "Suhasini was dead, yes, that was it, she was the one Mohan was mourning, she'd walked into the sea at last. No, the fact was that I'd finally done it—I'd killed her. No, that was not right, either; we had killed her between us, Mohan and I. But in dying she'd given me back the burden she'd been carrying for me all these years. I had finally to bear it myself, the burden of wifehood." (121) Herein lies the difference between Jaya's approach and that of a feminist who protests and, if necessary, leaves her husband's home. Jaya has felt that neither of the sexes can be eliminated from a healthy family or a healthy society. Hence the problems have to be solved through mutual discussion and not through silence or elimination. Jaya seems to accept the moral vision proposed by Robin Morgan:

> The women have over the centuries developed an ethic that is appropriate to the world view that is emerging out of the new physics: they see in terms of relationship and in terms of environmental of human values for centuries. Their primary value is a reverence for life. This ethic must become the governing world ethic.[12]

Deshpande the humanist desires a society which will treat both man and woman on equal terms, and in such a society feminism is not required.[13] In conclusion, the novelist's own remarks may be quoted:

> And then I wrote *That Long Silence*, almost entirely a woman's novel, nevertheless, a book about the silencing of one-half of humanity. A life time of introspection went into this novel, the one closest to my personality; the thinking and ideas in this are closest to my own.[14]

The readers would agree to the point that the writer is successful in reaching her goal and the novel is artistically perfect. Hence, as says Keki Daruwalla, a distinguished Indian poet, we need not bother much about the label to be imposed on the novel. To quote Daruwalla, "Labels are inadequate here, as they always are when confronting a work of art. One cannot dub *That Long Silence* either as a feminist or psychological novel. It has been written by a strong personality, a fine craftswoman and a novelist with an unerring eye for character."[15]

NOTES

1. Shashi Deshpande, Interviewed by Malini Nair, "The Message is Incidental," *Times of India*, No. 25, Nov. 1989.
2. Shashi Deshpande, "The Dilemma of a Woman Writer," *The Literary Criterion,* Vol. 20, No. 4, 1985.
3. *Ibid.*, p. 33.
4. Chaman Nahal, "Feminism in English Fiction: Forms and Variations," *Feminism and Recent Fiction in English,* pp.14-21.
5. Robin Morgan, *The Anatomy of Freedom: Feminism, Physics and Global Politics (*N.Y.: Doubleday, 1982), pp. 282-84.
6. Elaine Showalter defines 'female phase' as "a phase of self-discovery, a turning inward, freed from the dependence of opposition, a search for identity." *A Literature of Their Own : British Women Novelists from Bronte to Lessing (*Princeton, N.J.: Princeton University Press, 1977), p. 13.
7. Mohan did not accept Jaya's proposal that Kusum should be treated at Bombay. First he told that Kusum being no relation to her she need not bother about her. Then he continued, "I've always allowed you to do what you want. But this woman is not just sick, she is mentally sick. Is it wise to have her at home? Think of the children." (19) For the first time Jaya had really fought him, and finally put Kusum up in the Dadar flat.

   Kusum is here projected as Jaya's Other. In his seminal study, *Madness and Civilization,* Michel Foucault maintained that till the Renaissance, madness and reason used to work together. "But in less than half a century, it had been sequestered and, in the fortress of confinement, bound to Reason, to the rules of morality and to their monotonous nights." (*Madness and Civilization: A History of Insanity in the Age of Reason*, trans. Richard Howard [N.Y.: Vintage, 1973), p. 64. Foucault also insists that "the sane man could read in the madman, as in a mirror, the imminent movement of his downfall." (*Ibid.*, p. 248) Kusum's literal disappearance (her death) may be treated as a symbolic disappearance of the 'typical Indian mother figure,' of Jaya's spilt self.

   These characters are described by Sarla Palkar as "victims of patriarchy and also of their own silence." ("Breaking the Silence,

Shashi Deshpande's *That Long Silence*," *Indian Women Novelists*, Set 1, Vol. V, p. 166.

8. Thus Jaya on Mohan's reaction after her story about a couple was published: "I had known then that it hadn't mattered to Mohan that I had written a good story, a story about a couple, a man who could not reach out to his wife except through her body. For Mohan it had mattered that people might think the couple was us, that the man was him. To Mohan, I had been no writer, only an exhibitionist." (144)
9. Adele King, "Shashi Deshpande: Portraits of an Indian Woman," *The New Indian Novel in English: A Study of the 1980s*, ed. Viney Kirpal (New Delhi: Allied, 1990), p. 166.
10. Robin Morgan, pp. 282-84.
11. Toril Moi's observation may be recalled in this context: "In a non-sexist, non-patriarchal society, feminism will no longer exist." "Feminism, Postmodernism, and Style: Recent Feminist Criticism in the United States," *Cultural Critique*, 9 (Spring 1988), pp. 3-22.
12. Qtd. *Creative Theory: Writers on Writing (*Delhi: Pencraft International, 2000, ed. Jasbir Jain), p. 210.
13. "An Intense Book," Review of *That Long Silence, Indian Literature,* Vol. 34, No. 6, Nov.-Dec. 1991.

Realism in *That Long Silence*

Jaya, the protagonist in *That Long Silence*, is one of the rare narrative voices who possess remarkable literary sensibility as well as an awareness of the stifling social milieu. The curious point to note is that the novel is psychological, and the novelist's chief concern is to trace the protagonist's emergence from a comfortable position of a 'goody-goody' woman writer of a women's journal to one who is ready to pour out her innermost thoughts, ignoring the commotion she is going to create by letting loose her pent-up feelings. And yet, while revealing the truth behind man-woman relationship, a truth that she received through innermost experiences, the protagonist is not forgetful of the outer reality. Rather, she displays her well thought out concerns for the society, the setting around her. To quote the view of a critic, "Ostensibly, she (the narrator/writer) relates it as the story of a particular couple, but the power relations in the patriarchal structure, the gender differentiation with all its ramifications, and the typical travails of the woman struggling to define herself take on the dimension of the condition and place of the Indian woman in society."[1] The society is portrayed not as mere setting of the novel, but is rendered ironically, revealing the writer's critical attitude.

The protagonist Jaya was born on 3rd September 1939, and her father chose the name Jaya for her, proclaiming that 'Jaya' was for victory. Jaya passed her childhood in post-Gandhian days and through her recollections the blind alley of Indian politics is hinted at. That thousands of young Indians sacrificed their career at the call of Gandhiji, and were then abandoned by the mainstream of politics, becomes evident from the single case of Jaya's father. Jaya says,

> Appa [father] never had any doubts, he often told us, about the fact that victory would come, nor about whose victory it was going to be. He had given up his studies in Gandhi's name, burnt a few 'foreign' clothes and worn a Gandhi cap for a few years; but Churchill himself couldn't have been more certain of an ultimate Allied victory. (15)

Irony is blended with humour in the above passage. Jaya's father is rendered as an optimist and an idealist, but his failure in life indicates that the society is not yet prepared for persons like him.[2] After leaving Congress he joined *Hindu Mahasabha*, and had to face political death because of this decision. Through Jaya's remembrances a closed chapter of Indian history comes up with its photographic details:

> When we were children, my father was in the *Hindu Mahasabha*. And after Gandhi died he had to go into hiding, you remember how they were persecuted then because of Godse? And one day a mob came to loot our shop. My mother—we stayed above the shop—she kept crying, "My children will starve, don't do it, my children will starve." She tried to stop them, but they didn't, not until they had cleaned out the shop. And they called themselves Gandhians, those men who were after men like my father. Poor Gandhi, he thought he could change human nature, but people don't change. (180)

Even as a girl Jaya could feel the difference between façade and reality. The society openly looked down upon the film artists though almost everybody liked films. Even film songs were prohibited for the young ones. Jaya remembers how she was scolded by her father as she could not resist the urge for listening to the film songs sung by Lata and Rafi. When she becomes a mother, she finds that her son takes to comic books for some time, and then turns to cricket, then to music. This is taken up as quite natural. But Jaya's fascination for light music was seriously viewed by her father and the humiliation she felt, left a mark on her psyche, compelling her to face a trauma that arouses out of repression and humiliation. Makarandmama was reviled and abused by the members of his family and was virtually alienated from all, as he took up acting in film as his profession. But after his untimely death, his relatives began to express how they had appreciated him, presumably because they coveted to occupy his flat. Jaya says, "It's a pity he never knew how much they all admired him and sympathized with him behind that façade of hostility. For that is how they all made it out to be later—after the man's death." (43) Through this apparently innocent revelation, the middle class mentality—its greed, its lack of aesthetic sense and duplicity—is exposed.

Jaya heard others utter the most oft-quoted words of the Gandhian era—simple living and high thinking. She describes how the children in the family were denied any good dress or some other things of their liking in the name of this Gandhian motto.

> Simple living and high thinking—the words of the Gandhian era. The words I had heard so often as a child. Ramukaka's favourite axiom, repeated *ad nauseam* to any of his family who asked for something: "It's not how you look, what you have or what you wear that's important. Look at Gandhi . . . none of his children had dared retort, though they had grumbled privately, 'But we're not Gandhi." (60)

Through an incident of her life, Jaya shows that the people like Ramukaka, representing grown-up people in the Gandhian era, have been doing quite the opposite of what they would say. During her second pregnancy, she once started bleeding suddenly and went to hospital as she was, wearing her crumpled, soiled sari. As the doctor came to her side, he thought that a woman in such a dress would not understand English, and he started questioning in his convent-accented Hindi. He was using the simplest terms, "struggling to find the right words, simple enough to be understood by the kind of woman he had judged me to be from my appearance." (60) Much to the doctor's surprise, Jaya answered in English, not deliberately using the language but doing it automatically. "Suddenly his face had changed. He had looked young, foolish, at a terrible disadvantage. His air of superiority had oozed out, leaving him foolishly drooping." At that moment, the chief medical officer came and informed her that her husband had just rung. Later the young doctor apologized. Jaya asked why he should be sorry, feigning ignorance. But both of them knew what the matter was. The incident makes it clear that Gandhiji's message is used only as lip service, and that plain dress is not given due importance in the society.

Political incidents, war or agitation, which have been parts of Jaya's memory, are also described and these are perfectly blended with the psychological probing. When Mohan is talking about his hard labour in Lohanagar, Jaya is reminded of her busy schedule at the time and as Mohan demands an answer from her, she visualizes the enthusiastic picture of friendship between India and China, one that was followed by a war between the two countries. Jaya says,

> I could only see the girls in the hostel, all of us, standing on our balconies and watching the road—lining crowds wave flags and cheer the two men who folded their hands in a greeting and smiled blandly back. I heard the cries of '*Hindi-Chini bhai bhai.*' But almost immediately came the war. We had been stabbed by our 'brother.' Yes, that betrayal had been the watershed between hope and cynicism, between dreams and disillusionment. Things would never be the same again. (59)

It is because Jaya is endowed with both intellectual and literary qualities and is introduced as a good convent educated writer, it has been easy for the author to bring in outer reality, political and social, without disturbing the flow of the narrative. The outer reality is rendered as an indivisible part of Jaya's consciousness.

The record of Jaya's effort to assert her individuality also includes references to the scarcity of food and other necessary things in India before the days of Green Revolution. Jaya's children cannot even imagine the condition of suffering from food, as they have been used to affluence, and don't have the scope to experience what scarcity implies.

> When I spoke to them of how 'we never ate rice for months,' and 'even on Divali day, we didn't have a spoonful of sugar in the house,' they had stared at me blankly. I suppose these things didn't sound real to them, beneficiaries of the green revolution. Even to me, as I go about airily picking plastic bags of food from the loaded shelves of department stores, they seem like made-up stories. With this plethora about us, those days seem a fantasy. (71)

Differentiating scarcity from famine, Jaya further observes that famine brings to mind the image of parched lands, bloated corpses and vultures, while scarcity is queues—"people waiting in long queues for hours, for a minute bit of sugar, for a small quality of weevily rice from God knows where, for the almost inedible wheat given by the grace of America." (72)

Jaya's keen observation of the manmade poverty—of the countless persons losing jobs for strikes in the factories and their children dragged to the condition of beggars—is evident from the images of poverty strewn over the narrative structure. The incident of the children's taking ice cream cone on the Juhu beach may be quoted as an instance of Jaya's keen observation of the world outside and of her humanity:

> I sat in the car listening idly to the talk of the men while the children ran off to get their ice creams. When they returned with their cones, a few children followed them. They didn't seem to be professional beggars, for they were neither begging nor importuning; they only followed Rahul and Rati silently, their eyes following the cones unwaveringly as the children licked them, a hand cupped underneath to catch the drips. . . . I saw the emaciated bodies move in frantic quicksilver movements, I saw the deadly struggle, I saw

> the swiftness with which the victor disposed of the remnant of Rahul's cone, I saw the steadiness with which the others resumed their watch over Rati. (72-73)

And the narrator also informs that Bombay is overflowing with beggars as there is no rain and no crops. That the relief works are also provided by the government is known. When they go to cinema hall, the news reels show the picture of relief work:

> Men and women working under a blazing sun, carrying baskets of mud, chipping away at large slabs of stone. Much later I read that the road which these people had been constructing was never completed. And that a large number of those men and women, unused to stone chipping, had been blinded by tiny chips flying into their eyes. Nothing achieved but statistics in files. (74-75)

Jaya's consciousness is filled up with such images of the outer world—the images of stark reality that fill the reader's mind with anger and helplessness. The callousness and duplicity of the government and of those who belong to the affluent class are vividly exposed. The narrator being a member of the upper class, this exposure has been sharp and objective.

The ugly city life, the mobs and processions, the drab buildings and bad smell, and such other details are also inserted in the narrative, and help to make a fitting background for the protagonist's self-realization.

> Bombay, when I first came to it, had been a shock after the piquant contrasts of Saptagiri. In Saptagiri . . . our house had been surrounded by fruit orchards, and the clean little ribbon of a tarred road leading to it had been bordered by tamarind trees and gutters in which nothing ever ran but rain water.
>
> But Bombay, I'd realized at once, was nothing but a grey, uniform ugliness. The buildings had seemed terrible to me, endless rows of looking-exactly-alike, ramshackle, drab buildings, the washing that flapped on their balconies giving them a sluttishly gay look. It had taken me some time to notice the streets of Bombay; once I did, however, I had been immediately caught up by the

> magic of their teeming life. I had watched in utter fascination the mobs, the brawls, the drunkards, the school children, the coy newly-weds. And processions.

That Long Silence does not project the outer reality from a detached observer's viewpoint. The protagonist's concern for corruption, oppression, indifference and lack of human sensibilities are manifested in these descriptions.

Shashi Deshpande's approach to man-woman relationship also displays her strong sense of reality. Instead of portraying any idealistic picture of love and sex, she shows what actually happens in life when a well educated girl with literary sensibilities faces situations, utterly different from her idealistic views. Compelled by the pressure of circumstances she has to change her notions about love:

> Mohan. . . . I'd said the name to myself after we got married, but it had tasted unfamiliar. The man too—we were married, yet he was a stranger. Intimacy with him had seemed a grotesque indecency. Surely, I'd thought, it was not expected of me, not at once, anyway? We would achieve it gradually, by degrees or stages, I'd optimistically reassured myself.
>
> Whereas for Mohan it had been extremely simple. We were married, we were husband and wife, so everything, according to him, was permissible. He had taken it for granted that I thought the same way. And so perhaps it was only I who had been surprised when intimacy had come, all of a sudden, with the physical link. We had slipped into it with a precipitancy that had taken me unawares.
>
> The truth had been that if I was ignorant so was he; but somehow, after those first few days of clumsy fumbling, it had been suddenly all right. . . . Sensual memories are the coldest. They stir up nothing in you. As I thought of those days, of my feelings, and then looked at the man lying beside me, nothing stirred in me. Those emotions and responses seemed to belong to two other people, not to the two of us lying here together. (94-95)

The above passage reflects the idealistic views of a young woman. But when such a woman faces reality and gains experience, she is likely to change her views. Jaya also changes her view as she develops experiences. As she says, "First there's love, then there's sex—that was how I had always imagined it to be. But after living with Mohan I had realized that it could so easily be the other way round." (95) Through Jaya's changed feelings, Deshpande reveals her acute sense of reality. The importance of sexual life has been asserted by her, though she does not put undue emphasis on this aspect. With a realist's keen observation, she modifies Marx's view on man-woman relationship. The day Jaya runs away from Kamat not responding to his eagerness to have a physical contact, she is united with Mohan eagerly and reflects that Marx was wrong in his observation that a relation between a man and a woman is the most natural one. For, she now analyses her displaced passion and recognizes that her body wanted to respond to Kamat's call while the chain of marriage held her back. And her thwarted desire leads her to a mechanical contact which is by no means natural. Thus Deshpande exposes her experiences of the real world that includes both outer reality and inner reality.

NOTES

1. Subhash Chandra, "Silent No More: A Study of *That Long Silence*," *Indian Women Novelists*, ed. R.K.Dhawan (New Delhi: Prestige, 1991), Set 1, Vol. 1, p. 148.
2. Jaya's father started his political career as a follower of Gandhiji. He left his educational institution at Gandhi's call. But later he joined *Hindu Mahasabha*, a political organization opposed to the Indian National Congress. Though Jaya hardly makes a comment on her father's leaving one party for another, it is suggested that he was disappointed with the way the party was functioning. He did not try for a job, but opened his own business. After Gandhiji was killed, the small store owned by Jaya's father was destroyed by the

followers of Gandhi on the plea that he joined a political party opposed to the Congress. All these point at his failure in life. Moreover, his attempt to be a writer was also foiled. Jaya's mind would be burdened with sorrow whenever she looked at the unsold copies of his books waiting for being eaten up by white ants. He also died young.

Characterization in *That Long Silence*: The Protagonist's Self-Actualization

That Long Silence centres on the process of its protagonist's realizing herself. The difference between Deshpande's protagonist and say, the women characters in Margaret Laurence's writing, explains the former's distinct method of characterization. Margaret Laurence projects strong, active, sexually fulfilled and professionally successful women like Morag in *The Diviners* as she is a strong supporter of radical feminism.[1] Shashi Deshpande, on the other hand, chooses Jaya as her protagonist who apparently shows none of the qualities that form a radical feminist. Jaya is a writer endowed with artistic skill which is proved not only by Kamat's praise but also by Jaya's winning the first prize in a story writing competition. As is suggested by the theme of the story, Jaya embarked on the realistic method of delineating the man-woman relationship, but retreated from her stand; instead, she started writing about a woman's role as a mother and a wife, under the mythical name 'Seeta' in a women's journal. Her marital relationship with Mohan that she continued with much effort, also proved to be disappointing, and the possibility of her extra-marital relationship with Kamat was nipped in the bud. As a mother also, she failed to have knowledge about her children. Jaya's failure on each of the levels—professional, sexual and emotional—was a rude shock to her and after she has come over the initial shock, she starts self-analysis and finally gets ready to make her choice which, again, is different from a feminist protest against male supremacy.

Jaya's split personality becomes evident when she was looking through her old diaries in the Dadar flat, and was surprised to find little connections between her old self as revealed in the pages of the diaries and her present self:

> Looking through these diaries, I realized, was like going backwards. As I burrowed through the facts, what I found was the woman who had once lived here. Mohan's wife, Rahul's and Rati's mother. Not myself.
>
> But what was that 'myself'? 'Trying to find oneself'—what a cliché that has become. As if such a thing is possible. As if there is such a thing as one self, intact and whole, waiting to be discovered. On the contrary, there are so many, each self attached like a Siamese twin to a self of another person, neither able to exist without the other. (69)

The meticulous records in the pages of the diaries—the matter-of-fact prosaic report of the articles bought for the household, their price, the servants' absences, the advance payment they have taken and whatnot—only reveal the sensible particularity of the woman who had written these things. This is the same woman who was scared of cockroaches, lizards, nervous about electrical gadgets, hopeless at technical matters. This was a typical woman who was nervous, incompetent, needing male help and support. But Jaya was not always like this. Previously she was not so full of fears, not so afraid of darkness and insects. She remembers the peculiar exhilaration she had, while moving in a company car that passed through the "shouting, gesticulating menacing looking" labourers who were on strike. This fearlessness was due to the influence of Jaya's father who always told that she was different from others, that she would surely bring victory as is suggested by her name Jaya, meaning victory.

After her father's death Jaya could somehow complete her graduation course, thanks to the financial help provided by her maternal uncles. But she was married off soon, as her elder brother was eager to get relieved of the duty entrusted to him after his father's death. Her husband Mohan, an engineer in a steel plant, tried for a transfer in the Sales, and having been granted, settled in Bombay. During her brief stay at Mohan's home, Jaya was acquainted with a typical housewife's life though she did not take it up immediately. She discovered how sharply defined a woman's role was. As Jaya says, "I had never seen so clear, so precise a pattern before, and I had been entranced by it." It took some time, however, to get her adjusted to the new life and to eliminate those qualities which are disapproved by Mohan. Curiously, Jaya brings no charge of oppression against Mohan who even hardly shouted at her. He only expressed his disappointment and seemed hurt whenever Jaya would behave in a way not approved by him. Jaya remembers his reaction when she remarked like a stupid that his mother was a cook:

> His anger had at first taken me unawares. Then, getting the feel of it, I had met his anger with my own, deliberately using it as a weapon. Raging, furious, I had flung accusation wildly at him.
>
> As my own anger had grown, I had felt his dwindling, and finally I found myself raging at a silent, blank-faced man. I had ignored his silence at first, but when it had gone on, not for hours, but for days, it had unnerved me. It was I who had made the first conciliatory move and only then, when he had spoken to me, had I realized what my anger had done to him. It had shattered him. (81-82)

Jaya now realized the depth of her power over Mohan. But she was shaken by a distaste she had seen on his face when she had got into a temper. He looked at her as if anger had made her ugly. Later when she understood him better, she realized that according to him anger made woman 'unwomanly.' After that she learnt to control her anger lest she be 'unwomanly' to him. Jaya also confesses that being 'terrified' of his disapproval, she gradually developed womanly qualities. She began to be praised for these newly acquired qualities and became "ridiculously pleased."

Jaya's womanly qualities were totally disapproved only by Kamat, the lonely, elderly man of literary sensibilities, who happened to be her neighbour. Jaya remembers her conversation with Kamat one day, and her real motive that led her to be moulded as a woman, is mercilessly exposed:

> And when I had been praised for anything, I'd been so ridiculously pleased, 'I almost wag my tail, like a dog that's been patted by its master,' I had told Kamat.
>
> 'Don't try to act the martyr now. It's all your fault. You really enjoy it, don't you?'
>
> 'What?'
>
> 'Making others dependent on you. It increases sense of power. And that is what you really want, all your bloody looking-after-others, caring-for-others women.' (84)

It is Jaya's capacity for acute self-analysis that paves the way for making an independent choice.

Jaya's decision to write for a women's magazine under the mythical name of 'Seeta' is nothing but her attempt to gain cheap popularity and to please Mohan. She also equates her to Draupadi who followed her husband in exile. But her acute self-analysis compels her to admit that she is responsible for following the path of Seeta, and not of, say Maitreyee, the wife of the great philosopher Yajnavalkya. As Jaya says,

> The truth is that it was Mohan who had a clear idea of what he wanted, the kind of life he wanted to lead, the kind of home he would live in, and I went along with him. But I cannot blame Mohan, for even if he had asked me—what do you want?—I would have found it hard to give him a reply. Maitreyee comes to my mind now, Maitreyee who so definitely rejected her philosopher husband Yajnavalkya's offer of half his property. 'Will this property give me immortality?' she asked him. 'No,' he said, and

> she immediately rejected the property. To know what you want. . . . I have been denied that. (25)

Comparing herself to the sparrow in the story of the crow and the sparrow,[2] Jaya admits that she aspired for safety in choosing the life of a housewife, one who follows her husband without questioning, that is, without disturbing her own conscience. She also reflects on how the little girls are taught to be selfish through the story of the sparrow and the crow:

> They will store this story in their subconscious, their unconscious or whatever, and eventually they will become that damnably, insufferably priggish sparrow looking after their homes, their babies . . . and to hell with the rest of the world. Stay at home, look after your babies, keep out the rest of the world, and you're safe. That poor idiotic woman Suhasini [the name given to Jaya by Mohan] believed in this. I know better now. I know that safety is always unattainable. You're never safe. (17)

Jaya's sense of safety is shaken when Mohan is accused of malpractice in the office and apprehends loss of job. In addition to that, she is humiliated to hear from Mohan that he did it for the comfort of Suhasini and others in the family. Jaya cannot argue, as she knows that nothing will come out of her argument. The critical situation in her life reaches its climax when Mohan leaves the Dadar flat angrily, without telling her anything, and her son Rahul who was on a tour with another family, is reported to be missing. The outward crisis is over with Rahul's return and with the information from Mohan that his trouble is gone. But the internal crisis that has started with the process of Jaya's self-analysis is not over. That crisis has brought a total change in Jaya's life. Earlier she was afraid to be alone; but now she wants to remain alone, as she wants to be herself. She wants solitude because she has to decide what exactly she wants from life:

> 'I want immortality,' Maitreyee said. 'What do you want?' Nilima had asked me. I'd been so sure until now. If some one had asked

> me—what do you want?—I'd have given them an answer at once. Just to live. To know that at the end of the day my family and I are under a roof, safe, enclosed, in a secure world. If it's dark outside, what does it matter? I can close the door and windows, switch on the lights and the darkness will recede. But I know that I could never shut out the darkness; the darkness had invaded me. (181-82)

This realization that darkness has invaded her and that she is yet not afraid, marks the emergence of Jaya's new self and she is now able to confront reality.

Through the pattern of interior monologue, the writer has been able to highlight the change in Jaya. An effective use of mythical figures adds to her success. The myth of 'Seeta' may be compared to Paula Caplan's myth of 'suffering woman' which says that 'women enjoy their suffering.'[3] According to one myth described by Caplan, "there exists, like the diploma at the end of the course, a perfect, or perfectible, man for every woman who has learnt her skills. If he is not perfect, the fault must surely be in her, she has not learned to give or to suffer enough."[4] In this myth, as in the myth of motherhood, the woman is to be blamed, no matter what actually happens. In Indian mythology, Seeta is the incarnation of suffering. Whatever happens, she is always blamed and she gets relief only after her sacrifice. And yet, Seeta has been set as an example of womanhood. Jaya's decision to write under the name of 'Seeta' pleased her husband as well as other members in the society who believed in the myth of suffering woman. Women writers are supposed to be exhibitionists. The society does not like expressions of sexual life from a woman writer, no matter how much artistic it is. When Jaya realizes this after her encounter with Mohan who interpreted her story on man-woman relationship as a humiliating revelation of their own life, she did not choose the path of confrontation. Instead, she became contributor to a women's magazine, writing imaginary stories about imaginary persons. She felt that it was like the suicide of her writer's self, and yet she was lacking in courage required for confrontation. During her stay in the Dadar flat, thanks to Mohan's snub, she seriously tried to come out of the protective shell of Seeta.

> Perhaps he thought I was doing my fortnightly 'Seeta' story. But suddenly 'Seeta' had exploded. There was nothing left of her, not even bits and pieces that could be put together. The month's deadline was long past. I could imagine them frantically trying to contact me, their angry mutterings as they failed to get me. It gave me pleasure to think of the blank page where 'Seeta' would have been. But of course there would be no blank page. There never could be one. There would be something replacing 'Seeta.' (69)

Even when Jaya was continuing her writings for 'Woman's World,' she knew that she was writing about unreal matters:

> That column, yes, it had made me known. My profile silhouetted in stark black that accompanied each article frightened me each time I saw it. It was like seeing someone masquerading as myself, or as if I was masquerading as the woman who wrote that column. The woman who wrote this had no doubts about anything, only strong convictions. And she was a liberal, without any prejudices. (119)

Though Jaya stopped writing those trash matters, she is yet to find out her goal as a writer. Only when the process of her self-realization is complete and she acquires necessary courage, she is able to exercise her freedom of choice and she is expected to start writing on her own. Her failure as a writer was due to her own fault: she was just afraid to face the readers and particularly, her husband. Now that she possesses moral courage to justify her stand and that she is no more expecting 'safety,' she is prepared to speak out the butt-ends of her days and ways.

Jaya's failure in making love relationship is also highlighted in the novel. During the early years of her married life she developed frenetic emotions towards Mohan, though she felt ashamed of her emotional extravagances. She tried to rationalize her feelings in the following way:

> We are all frightened of the dark, frightened of being alone. And so we cling to one another, saying 'I love you, I want you, I need you.' Often I had told myself: love is a myth, without which sex with the same person for a life time would be unendurable. Sometimes, like the time I read an American poet's confession of her guilt because she just couldn't get along without her husband, it had seemed hopeless—I would never be able to shake off this monstrous burden. (97)

She understood later that 'time' took away the agony out of her feelings for Mohan. Reflecting on her 'loneliness' just after a physical union with him, Jaya says:

> But, lying there, my body still warm and throbbing from the contact with his, it had come to me in one awful moment—that I was alone. The contact, the coming together, had been not only momentary, but wholly illusory as well. We had never come together, only our bodies had done that. I had begun to cry then, despairingly, silently, scared that I would wake Mohan up, trying desperately to calm myself.
>
> Man and woman—it was then that I realized the deep chasm between the two. They are separated forever, never more than at the moment of total physical togetherness. (98)

Jaya also feels that they have never owned the vocabulary of love which, she thought, would come to them naturally and inevitably. Theirs is the vocabulary of the workaday world, she admits. (117) Jaya, yet, could come very close to the language of love; but ironically, she could not accept it, as it came from some 'prohibited area.' Marriage being a taboo for her she could not respond to Kamat's call. When she needed comfort—as after her father's death—she rushed to Kamat: "There were no more words and suddenly I had realized I was crying and he was holding me. But it had meant nothing. It had been warm and comforting, like wearing Appa's coat on a chilly night, like sitting before him on his bike. And then he had said 'Jaya' and I had looked up and seen it was not Appa. Oh God, it was not

Appa. And it was not Kamat either, the man to whom I'd been telling all these things. It had frightened me to find myself with this stranger. I had made a quick flurried movement as if to get away from him, but it had been he who had released me first." (156) This was Jaya's first experience of reaching at the threshold of love though she could not understand it.

Later, whenever she faced any awkward situation, she went straight to Kamat who brought back her lost faith on herself. 'Your name is like your face,' he once said to Jaya, passing his fingers lightly over her face. It was Kamat, again, who criticized her ideas as reflected in her writings, and pointed out the defects. He brought confidence in her mind and asked her to take herself seriously. He once told her, "Why didn't you use that anger in your story? There's none of it here. There isn't even a personal view, a personal vision. I'll tell you what's really wrong with your story. It's too restrained. Spew out your anger in your writing, woman, spew it out." (147) When the 'Seeta' column was published, Kamat called it an 'obnoxious creation,' and held that Jaya was meant for something higher. Jaya recalls her last meeting with Kamat when Kamat came very close to her and she left him without a word:

> His eyes had looked steadily, almost dispassionately at me. And my body had responded to that look, that voice, that touch. I had almost felt his body on mine, I had almost been able to smell and taste his lips.
>
> The body's response is so much simpler, so much more direct; is it possible that it is therefore more likely to be right? Even now I have no answer to that. At that moment, however, I had instantaneously rejected the body's response. I had moved away from him, from that scarcely touching grasp, I had left him without a word.
>
> There had been no anger in me when I had done that; there had been no outrage either. There had been nothing but an overwhelming urge to respond to him with my body, the equally overwhelming certainty of my mind that I could not do so (157)

This was Jaya's last meeting with Kamat. Some days later when she went to him, he was dead, "glassy-eyed, foul-smelling and dead." It was only after Mukta revealed to her how Kamat, who was her husband's friend, had helped her (Mukta) to be independent when she became widow, and accused Jaya of leaving him alone in his death-bed, Jaya could realize how her spirit had been chained to his. Mukta says,

> 'He was frightened of dying, Jaya, he was afraid of being alone. You could have been with him, you could have stayed by his side, but you didn't, you just walked away; he could have been lying there for days, he could have just rotted there if he hadn't given me the keys, if I hadn't gone there that day. He was a very lonely man, Jaya, didn't you ever think of that? He was terribly lonely, specially after his son went away.'
>
> I knew it now. 'Jaya,' he had said, and I had run away. He tried to reach out to me in his loneliness and it had frightened me. I'm Mohan's wife, I had thought, I'm only Mohan's wife, and I had run away. (186)

Jaya shares the suffering with Mukta, and realizes that her 'unnatural' attempt to accept one fragment of her self (Mohan's wife) as the only reality at the cost of suppressing the other selves, has resulted in split personality. She now accepts the burden of the sin of leaving one alone in his death-bed.

> The loneliness of a man facing his death—is there anything like it in this world? His pain filled this room and we could both of us feel it, Mukta and I. The fellowship of pain seemed to bind us together; we were like two patients in a hospital, suffering from the same disease, lying on two adjacent beds. (186)

Acceptance of the responsibility of sin paves the way for self-realization on the basis of which an individual chooses the way of his/her life. Jaya's confession to herself that she has wronged, enables her to assess her activities in an unbiased way:

> I tried painfully to retrace my way back through the disorderly, chaotic sequence of events and non-events that made up my life. It was like looking through the eyehole of the magic peepshow of my childhood. '*Raja dekho, Rani Dekho,*' the man would call out enticingly. 'Come and see the kings and queens.' And now I found myself looking at the picture of a girl, a child, wearing a dress with pockets for the first time, thrusting her hands in them, feeling heady with the excitement of finding unexpected resources within herself. That child was me. (187)

The unexpected resource that Jaya finds in her is her capacity to do what she desires. She remembers the Sanskrit words in her father's diary—*Yathecchasi tatha kuru*—meaning 'Do as you desire,' the words that were taken from the *Bhagavad Gita*. The words of Lord Krishna to his disciple-friend, Arjuna, put emphasis on the necessity of making choice. He gave knowledge to Arjuna all about the indestructible souls and desireless action, and made it clear that the course of action was not to be dictated. Action is always to be chosen by the individual; otherwise it will not be action proper. Earlier Jaya did not choose for her. Whenever Mohan asked her view on anything, she would just look at his face for clues, and then give him the answer she knew he wanted. But it is no more possible for her now; she will have to speak and to erase thereby the silence between them. In Sanskrit drama, she remembers, women characters were not allowed to speak Sanskrit. They had to use Prakrit instead. Jaya feels that it is as if she used 'Prakrit' in her writings. Time is up now for using 'Sanskrit.' That means, she has now acquired moral strength to face reality even at the cost of losing comfort and security.

That Long Silence thus renders a unique character sketch of its protagonist through the projection of suffering that the protagonist undergoes while realizing her true self. Jaya's dealings with her previous life—her pretences that she should have behaved only as Mohan's wife, which was taken to be her only identity after marriage—may be compared with Sartre's concept of 'bad faith.' According to Sartre, all sorts of pretences, pretentiousness and wilful ignorance are obstacles to free choice, and are therefore morally bad.[5] Man is condemned to be free, wrote Sartre, and yet man does not exercise his freedom as he is afraid to come out of his comfortable life and face the reality. Almost in a similar way Jaya opted for comfort and safety as she was lacking in moral courage to face the reality; and only after she becomes fully aware of her past role and takes the responsibility of choice, she emerges as an individual, not just as a woman moulded by society.

NOTES

1. When it emerged as a powerful movement, Feminism appeared monolithic. But gradually, it has been marked by contradictions and is now being located as a field of different discourses each with its unique understanding of the role of women in family, society and the state. Within feminism one can easily say what is wrong than say what is right or what liberation for ali women actually means. Critics, however, like to interpret these as differences within Feminism. Barbara Johnson, for example, says, "To say, for instance, that the difference between man and woman is an illusion created by the repression of differences within each, may to some extent be true." *A World of Difference* (Baltimore: Johns Hopkins, 1987), p. 8.
2. Jaya remembers the story of the sparrow and the crow heard in her childhood as a bed-time story. This is the story of the wise sparrow who built her nest of wax in which no one was allowed even during calamities. The foolish crow in the story had his nest made of dung which was washed away during rain. Shivering and sodden in the cold, the crow knocked on the door of the sparrow's house and requested her to let him in. The sparrow kept him waiting saying that she was feeding her babies and spinning other excuses. At last she opened her door to let him in. As the crow entered, she pointed to the hot pan where she had been preparing chapattis, and asked him to get warm on it. The foolish, gullible crow hopped on it and was burnt to death. Jaya wonders how such an ugly, sadistic story

could be told to children. Its effect on the girl children might have been terrifying, she says. "They will store this story in their subconscious, their unconscious or whatever, and eventually they will become that damnably, insufferably priggish sparrow looking after their homes, their babies, and to hell with the rest of the world. . . . Stay at home, look after your babies, keep out the rest of the world, and you're safe." (17)

3. *The Myth of Women's Masochism* (New York: E.P. Dutton, 1985), p. 1.
4. *Ibid.*, p. 102.
5. *Being and Nothingness*, trans. Hazel E. Barnes (London: Methuen, 1972), p. 49.

Character of Jaya

Jaya is the protagonist of the novel and she is by profession a writer. Here is therefore a unique opportunity for Shashi Deshpande to sketch a character who records the inner developments of a writer's soul. Moreover, Jaya being a woman writer, Deshpande gets a scope to clarify her attitude to feminist writers through Jaya's reflections. It is curious to note that Jaya's development as a writer runs parallel with her development as a human being. Being a woman Jaya takes up two women characters from the Hindu myths to suggest how her role in life gets changed. These two characters are Sita and Maitreyee. Jaya was at the beginning a woman like Sita who never questioned her husband. Gradually she developed firmness of character to acquire the capacity of questioning and of facing rude facts of life.

"To achieve anything, to become anything, you've got to be hard and ruthless." With these words the novel *That Long Silence* starts and these words throw light on Jaya's changed view of life. If one wants to be a saint and to love the whole world, as it is further clarified in the beginning of the novel, one has to stop loving individuals. Jaya did not want to be a saint, but just a loving housewife, and that too after her sudden marriage with an engineer. When she thought of starting a career of a writer, she could not be hard and ruthless. That is why she could not oppose her husband who found fault with her prize-winning story written on man-woman relationship, though she knew it very well that her husband Mohan was unable to get at the essence of the story. As Jaya records, that day Mohan came back from work carrying a magazine which he thrust on her saying that there was her story. Turning over the pages Jaya found that the story sent by her to a competition had won a prize and was published. Jaya was naturally much excited at this success, but Mohan's face was grave and he just wondered how she could bring into public their personal affair.

> 'They will all know now, all those people who read this and know us, they will know that these two persons are us, they will think I am this kind of a man, they will think I am this man. How can I look anyone in the face again? And you, how could you write these things, how could you write such ugly things, how will you face people after this?'
>
> I had realized it then, even in the state I have been in, that he had not been angry, but hurt; he had looked as if I wounded him. (144)

Jaya knew that it did not matter to Mohan that she had written a good story about a man who could not reach out to his wife except through his body. It only mattered to him that people might think that the man and woman in the story were Mohan and Jaya. And yet she could not argue with him on the topic lest he felt more hurt. That is, she could not be hard and ruthless; rather, she stopped writing any realistic story and failed to be a writer. Her next attempts were her imaginary stories regarding the lives of the housewives meant for the column 'Seeta' in a magazine. Though these stories were very much liked by the common public and by Mohan also, earning 'literary' fame for her, Jaya was aware that they carried no literary value. During her stay in the Dadar flat when she received some rude shocks from Mohan, she began to prepare herself for the career of a real writer who is devoted to the revelation of reality without bothering if he/she becomes rude in the process. Jaya is thus portrayed as a dynamic figure who can change her character and accept the responsibility of that change.

The distinguishing trait of Jaya's character is her humanity. She is far from all sorts of narrow interests, greed and jealousy. She took the responsibility of Kusum's treatment and arranged the Dadar flat for her stay during the treatment, going against Mohan's will. When her Vanitamami became ill, she felt it to be her responsibility to look after the childless widow. During her stay in the Dadar flat even when she was wretched both physically and mentally, she went to the hospital on her maidservant's request for meeting the doctor who was in charge of the treatment of the maid's step-son. Jaya did not like snobbery and felt uncomfortable among the snobs. Mohan complained that Jaya had never understood the necessity of chatting with his boss's wife. The works that she wanted to do but could not because of Mohan are also instances of her broadmindedness. She wanted to join a rally, to take a job and to adopt a baby. She was not childless and yet she wanted to adopt an orphan. This is an instance of her benevolent nature. Jaya's sympathy for all sorts of distressed people is manifested in the novel.

Jaya was secular in her approach to religion. The description of the idols of lord Ganapati reveals her attitude:

> there was a steady flow of Ganapatis on the road in a bizarre multiplicity of shapes and sizes. We stood at the edge of the pavement, unable to cross because of a huge procession that was held up for a girl who rushed out of a building, a plate of offerings in her hands. The men around the idol stopped, one of them devoutly accepted the plate, showered the god with flowers and broke the coconut at the edge of the pavement. Meanwhile the dancers leading the procession went on dancing.
>
> I watched them, feeling detached and remote from the scene; the gyrating, cavorting men became flat cardboard figures, and the whole scene took on the colour of absurdity. All this frenzied excitement for an elephant-trunked, pot-bellied, painted clay figure? If it was faith that created God—who had said that?—was such an extravagant, boisterously loud statement of faith needed then to keep this god alive? The meaning of it somehow eluded me. It was like a word seen over and over again, becoming finally just a meaningless jumble. (163-64)

This is the view of a rationalist who never supports any public hazard in the name of religion.

As a mother Jaya's role was hardly perfect. She failed to form the character of her daughter Rati who did not share her mother's views. With Rahul also Jaya could not develop a friendly relation at the beginning and thus it is found that Rahul preferred to go to his uncle's place when he could not anymore adjust himself to the family of his father's friend. However, Jaya's assurance and her sympathetic attitude to her son developed their relationship at the end of the novel. Jaya's relationship to Kamat remains an enigma. Much older than Jaya, Kamat helped her in all possible ways; but Jaya could not return that friendship. She could not dare to hold his hand even, when he stretched out his hands out of desperate fear for being alone at the time of death. Of course, Jaya had no idea that Kamat was dying, but the way she left him could not be supported. Jaya herself could find out the real cause of her behaviour. It was a social cause. When Mukta asked her if she were afraid of Mohan while leaving Kamat, the truth occurred to Jaya. "Stumbling over the words, I suddenly realized—it was not Mohan but marriage that had made me circumspect." (187)

Jaya's capacity of self-analysis is the distinguishing quality in her character. She has the courage to acknowledge her flaws. That is why she said that she did not intend to make Mohan a scapegoat. Thanks to her ruthless self-analysis, she knew that her fear of losing the comfort of a happy family was at the root of taking the role of 'Seeta.'

> Why had I suppressed that desperate woman? And now once again the man Nair and his family come back to me, that family that bound itself together and walked into the sea. We've been like that, all of us, bound by fear. Yes, I have been scared, scared of breaking through that thin veneer of a happy family. (191)

After the process of self-analysis was complete, Jaya became fearless. She was no more afraid of anything. The panic was gone. Earlier she thought that she was Mohan's wife and cut off the bits of her that had refused to be Mohan's wife. After she analysed her self she felt that that kind of fragmentation was not possible.

Character of Mohan

Mohan is a typical man of the materialistic world that is concerned only with physical comforts. A self-centred man, he thinks himself to be the centre of his world and ignores the existence of others. He was born in a very poor family and had to try hard to shine in life. He took monetary help from one rich, old man. Once, the man took him to a marriage party and Mohan went there against his will. In his world he had never seen fashionable English-educated ladies. In the marriage party three such girls caught his attention and captured his imagination. He was pitied by others and could hardly get any respect in the society at that time but he could not forget the glimpse of the girls and cherished a secret desire of marrying such a convent-educated girl. His desire was fulfilled later, when he could establish himself as an engineer. But it was not the work of fate; it was his tenacity that enabled him to get whatever he wanted. As Jaya could understand, Mohan has always had very clear ideas about himself. He was a dutiful man, a dutiful son, a dutiful husband. It is a matter of pity that though he had a good number of qualities, he was lacking in moral sense. He took it for granted that he had to arrange some extra money for getting more comforts in life, no matter if he had to adopt some immoral ways. He bluntly said to Jaya that it was for her and the children that he adopted illegal ways for getting more money. There being no poetic justice, Mohan was not punished. This is an example of the corruption going on in the third world countries like India.

That Long Silence as an Indian Novel

That Long Silence is an Indian novel not only because its setting is an Indian metropolis (Bombay) and its characters are typical Indians, but also because the essence of Indian thought and philosophy is introduced through its protagonist. Jaya, the protagonist, has an easy access both to Western literature and to the Indian classics. As a writer by profession, she represents postcolonial Indian writers in English, and is burdened with a double legacy. A convent-educated girl in an Indian city, Jaya has developed mastery on English language; and her literary sensibilities blended with a hold on reality, prepared her for a literary career. Born and brought up in a middle-class Hindu family, Jaya is well acquainted with the typical Indian characters and their approaches to life. When such a character becomes the protagonist of a novel, and the theme of the novel is self-revelation through self-analysis, the novelist has the privilege to introduce Indian thoughts and philosophy in a convincing way.

Through a long interior monologue that blurs the distinction between past and present, Jaya projects herself in four different roles. All these roles refer to the Indian classics and myths: the role of Sita (The *Ramayana*), of Draupadi (The *Mahabharata*), of Gandhari (The *Mahabharata*), and of Maitreyee (The *Upanishads*). Jaya starts with the role of Sita, the wife of Lord Shri Ram Chandra in the great Sanskrit epic, the *Ramayana*. For the Hindus, the *Ramayana* is not just an epic, and Ram and Sita only two characters in that epic. Sita had been accepted as the model wife in the Indian society since perhaps the days of her inception. She is suffering incarnate, and yet she never protested.

The myth of Sita, popular among the Indians, is being 'reconstructed' by some feminists who follow the principles of radical feminism. There are several instances of the reconstruction of the popular myths of female figures in world literature. Kim Chernin's *Reinventing Eve* is an example of reconstruction of the myth of Eve. Chermin observes that the modern woman who is in search of herself, "will not let herself be tricked into believing Eve is a whore, a great sinner."[1] Through the apple, Eve is associated with Gaea, the Greek earth mother, Idun, goddess of apple land in Norse mythology, and the Celtic queen of the dead in Avalon, who gave out apples for eternal life. Associated with life-giving powers, renewal, rebirth, transformation and the mystery of death, these gods are quite different from the passive Eve of the Biblical myth. Margaret Atwood's reworking of Greek myth in her Circe poems is another example of women's interaction with myths. Deshpande does not attempt any such reworking of the myth of Sita. She projects her protagonist in the role of Sita as long as she feels comfortable in that role. And when the role does not suit her changed sensibilities, she rejects that role and goes for another, as there is no scarcity of role models in Indian myths.

Jaya's playing the role of Sita serves a double purpose. At home the role of Sita is appreciated by her husband and the relatives, and Jaya receives applause and also a sense of security. As for her career, the role of Sita helps her find a corner in a women's magazine to which she regularly contributed, much to the satisfaction of Mohan. The role of Sita demanded sacrifice: Jaya had to sacrifice her individuality and had to mould her as per Mohan's desire. She cut her long hairs, did not go for a job, aborted against her will, and among many other things, ceased to be a self-conscious writer with an urge for exposing reality. She later tried to give Mohan a list of occasions when she was subdued:

> The job I wanted to take, the baby I had wanted to adopt, the anti-price campaign I'd wanted to take part in. . . . But even as I listed these to myself, it came to me that perhaps it had nothing to do with Mohan, the fact that I had not done these things, that I had left them alone. Perhaps I had not really cared enough about these things myself. Instead I said, and my voice sullen even to me, 'I've done everything you wanted me to.' (120)

Jaya's approach reveals a typical Indian attitude. When a Hindu girl marries, she knows that it is bondage of souls and she is expected to merge her will in the will of her husband. Jaya tried to do what exactly she was expected to do by her husband and also by the society.

The feminist critics would interpret such passages as examples of compromise, as they fail to delve deep beneath the surface.[2] Any of the cases from Jaya's list would have provoked the feminists to start campaign against the suppression of women in the male dominated society. Jaya did not do so as she had embraced the Indian tradition consciously, and had recognized that if anything she had to do, it was to bring a change in Mohan's mind, which was next to impossible. Human nature does not change, she said.

When a critic brings the charge that Deshpande writes not as the champion of the Indian women, but as their articulator,[3] that critic appears to tread on the surface. Deshpande delved deep in her analysis of the Indian tradition and found that it is the development of consciousness that matters ultimately. Hence, her protagonist did not choose the way of running to the street with catchy slogans, made familiar by the radical feminists. She followed the path of the Indian philosophers who put emphasis on consciousness. Some familiar axioms in India may be quoted: *Atmanang Viddhi* (know thyself); *Atmadeepa Bhava* (Be your own light), *Twat Tam Asi* (Thou art Him). It is emphasized in all these sayings that human consciousness is the supreme reality, and that, through the development of consciousness man may reach the region of the Almighty. Therefore, Deshpande chooses a course of the rigorous process of self-realization for her protagonist. In order to analyze oneself, it is necessary to get detached from one's own self. Jaya is an expert in this art and she judges her previous selves as actors assigned to particular set roles.

Jaya's role as Sita was all pervasive. Once she took up that role, she had to continue despite her dissatisfaction with the role. Jaya accepted Mohan as her 'profession,' her 'career,' and her 'means of livelihood.' She began to feel that life without Mohan would be meaningless for her. His desires and approval seemed to be the most important thing for her life, as it was for Sita in the ancient days. In the modern context Jaya had also to follow the advice of the fashion magazines in order to be a *saddhi* (the follower of one's husband). As she finds in retrospect,

> There had been a time—it came back to me—when I had so faithfully followed all the edicts laid down by the women's magazines. They had been my Bible, and I had pored over the wisdom contained in them. *Don't let yourself go. How to keep your husband in love with you. Keep romance alive in a marriage. The quality of charm in a woman. . . .* Where dos it come from? . . .
>
> Years later, long after I had given up all these exercises, the thought had come to me: it was ridiculous, he would have slept with me faithfully twice a week whether I creamed my face or not, whether I brushed my hair a hundred times or not, whether I wanted him to or not—yes, there had been that too. Yet, I had always been apprehensive of not pleasing him as a woman. (96-97)

Jaya's dissatisfaction with the role of Sita is marked by her awareness that her feelings towards Mohan were not reciprocated. The questioning self could no more be suppressed. Earlier she could not even think of being separated from Mohan, but after a period of time she began to feel that she could stay apart from him without a twinge. During this time she felt that love is a myth, and yet she continued to stay with Mohan as usual. Falsity pervades the scene now, compelling her to realize that she is lying to herself.

Jaya's role as a faithful wife of Mohan (as Sita was faithful to Rama) is supplemented by her role of a writer, a contributor to a woman's magazine. In both the cases she was not taking herself seriously. Her relationship with Mohan was not natural, but mechanical. And her writing did not bear the mark of her personality. As Kamat said to her, those writings could be owned by any one. In her 'Seeta' column, she was writing about a housewife's problems which were imaginary and trash. During this time Jaya took up, simultaneously, the role of Gandhari, the mother of one hundred 'Kauravas' and the wife of the blind king Dhritarashtra. Since the day of her marriage, Gandhari had used a covering on her eyes so that she might be denied eyesight like Dhritarashtra. Dhritarashtra's loss of physical eyesight was also accompanied by his moral blindness. His love for his children also made him blind to their faults. Gandhari's feigned blindness also kept her unaware of the criminal acts committed by her sons and supported by her husband. She just did not exercise her knowledge of good and evil. Almost in the way Gandhari chose to remain blind, Jaya also posed to be blind, not bothering about the ways adopted by Mohan for getting a better quarter and then a transfer to Bombay. Jaya says,

> Mohan had managed to get the job (a non-technical post in the purchase section, in Bombay). I never asked him how he did it. If Gandhari, who bandaged her eyes to become blind like her husband, could be called an ideal wife, I was an ideal wife too. I bandaged my eyes tightly. I didn't want to know anything. It was enough for me that we moved to Bombay, that we could send Rahul and Rati to good schools, that I could have the things we needed . . . decent clothes, a fridge, a gas connection, traveling first class. And there was enough for Mohan to send home to his fa-

> ther—for Sudha's fees, Vasant's clothes and Sudha's marriage. (61-62)

Jaya was perfectly doing the role of Gandhari, without bothering about moral good and evil. She had taken her position as Mohan's wife for granted, and ceased to be an individual who exercises her power of discrimination between the good and the evil. Only when Mohan brought the accusation that he did malpractice for Jaya and the family, Jaya was crestfallen. She had never imagined that she would have to take the responsibility of Mohan's misdeeds. This time also she did not let loose her anger, but started introspection. There was also a side role, that of Draupadi, which merged with the role of Sita when Jaya followed Mohan in the Dadar flat. When their husbands were in trouble, both Sita and Draupadi followed them in exile. Almost in the same way, Jaya followed Mohan.

Jaya's self-analysis revealed to her that she could very well take the role of Maitreyee who rejected her husband's wealth on the ground that wealth would not lead to immortality. The fact is that Jaya was not prepared for making a choice of her own. It requires moral courage and a total hold on one's self when one makes a free choice. Jaya was lacking in both, and so she was unprepared for choice. Hence, only a passive role could suit her. Her own self is revealed to her only after she was left to her introspection in the Dadar flat.

> The truth is that it was Mohan who had a clear idea of what he wanted, the kind of life he wanted to lead, the kind of home he would live in, and I went along with him. But I cannot blame Mohan, for even if he had asked me—what do you want?—I would have found it hard to give him a reply. Maitreyee comes to my mind now, Maitreyee who so definitely rejected her philosopher husband Yajnavalkya's offer of half his property. 'Will this property give me immortality?' she asked him. 'No,' he said, and she immediately rejected the property. To know what you want. . . . I have been denied that. (25)

Jaya further says that in answer to Maitreyee's query, Yajnavalkya told her that her life would be like anyone else's if she took his wealth. The idea of immortality still appeared crazy to her. But when her self-scrutiny was completed, Jaya became full of courage and got ready for choosing the course of her life. Finally, Jaya is prepared for taking up the role of Maitreyee when she says that she will break the silence between Mohan and her. Maitreyee was not silent; she dared to question her philosopher husband and after a series of conversation she got what she had aspired for. When Jaya thinks of taking up the role of Maitreyee, she has already decided to break the silence between Mohan and her. Thus, the novel may be described as Jaya's progress from a passive role to an active one. Putting aside the role of Sita and Gandhari, Jaya comes out prepared for taking the role of Maitreyee. Deshpande is to be credited for utilizing the resources of Indian myths for projecting her protagonist's 'pilgrim's progress.'

Before taking up the role of Maitreyee Jaya had to emerge out of her selfish self, one that was likened to the sparrow in the story of the crow and the sparrow. The sparrow in that Indian tale was a mother of babies and lived in a nest made of wax which was safe during rain. The crow lived in a mud-built nest which got melted during rain, and he came to the sparrow's nest for shelter. The selfish sparrow did not let him in for a long time, and when, at last, the crow was allowed to enter, he was shown the stove for making him warm. The foolish crow sat on the stove and was burnt. Jaya felt that she was like the sparrow in the story who had acted in a selfish way only to remain safe[4]. But one cannot remain safe forever. The investigation against Mohan's alleged malpractice and the fear of his being sacked had rudely shaken Jaya's sense of safety, and now Mohan's accusation that Jaya was responsible for his malpractice, shattered the illusion that Jaya had been maintaining so long. The roles of Sita and Gandhari did not fit in in her changed sensibilities. The only role available to her is the role of Maitreyee who did not bother about safety and did not require her husband's wealth either.

That Long Silence is a serious novel that deals with the problem of good and evil, and of sin and retribution. The incident that aroused the conscious process of Jaya's self-realization was that of an investigation into Mohan's malpractice. The incident exposed the facts that Mohan's greed for material prosperity got the better of his moral sense, and that he even had the audacity to make others responsible for his sin. (He said to Jaya that he had done it for her and the family). It is also exposed that Jaya also maintained wilful ignorance, not bothering to know how Mohan arranged all sorts of comforts in life. She has to face her own self and has to admit that she was used to the cosy life arranged by Mohan and did not just like to disturb her sheltered life through uncomfortable questions. If Mohan is a sinner, Jaya too, has to be one. Her enlarged consciousness must not spare her. All these thoughts lurk behind her mind, as she starts introspection. This concern with good and evil and with sin and retribution is a characteristic quality of Indian classics to have a clear idea of which the readers are required to have an insight into Indian ethos. As Jaya says,

> There was a simple word I had to take into account: retribution. How ajji had frightened us children with her dire pronouncements—'Tell lies now and you'll be a lizard in your next life, steal things and you'll be a dog, cheat people and you'll be a snake.' Now I knew better. We didn't have to wait for another life for our punishment. It was all reserved for us right here and now. An act and retribution—they followed each other naturally and inevitably. Dasarath killed an innocent young boy whose parents died crying out for their son. And years later, Dasarath died too, calling out for his son, 'Rama Rama.' (127-28)

This is an Indian sensibility, and the reader is expected to know the story of King Dasharath in the *Ramayana*.

At the last stage of her self-realization, Jaya is reminded of the remarks of Lord Shri Krishna in the *Bhagavad Gita*. On the battlefield of Kurukshetra, Lord Shri Krishna told Arjuna all about the different ways of worship and about the illusory views of life. Lastly, Shri Krishna told that Arjuna himself would have to make his choice. *Yathecchasi tatha kuru*—'Do as you desire.' Jaya did not understand it earlier. But now she feels the implication of Arjuna's remark:

> But now I understand. With this line, after those millions of words of instruction, Krishna confers humanness on Arjuna. 'I have given you knowledge. Now you make the choice. The choice is yours. Do as you desire.' (192)

It becomes clear to Jaya that in order to assert her individuality she is to make a choice of her own. Maitreyee made a choice of her own. She did not just accept the wealth conferred on her by her husband. She questioned him and there followed a long discourse. Her questions were not mere rhetoric. They emerged out of the depth of her mind and they enabled her to make her choice perfect. At the last stage of her self-analysis, Jaya also learns how to make a choice of her own. Her newly realized self can no more play the role of unquestioning Sita:

> Mohan will be back. 'All well,' his telegram says. Does he mean by this that we will go back to being 'as we were'? Does it mean that, now that Mohan has sorted out his problem, and no longer fears prosecution, joblessness and disgrace, we can go back to our original positions? Does it mean that he will come back and give me a carefully edited version of what has happened—as he has done so often till now—and then ask me, 'What do you say, Jaya?'
>
> Until today, this has been a rhetorical question. I have looked at his face for clues and then given him the answer I knew he wants, I have only to do this now and authority will seep into Mohan once more.
>
> But it is no longer possible for me. If I have to plug that 'hole in the heart,' I will have to speak, to listen, I will have to erase the

> silence between us. While studying Sanskrit drama, I'd learnt with a sense of outrage that its rigid rules did not permit women characters to speak Sanskrit. They had to use Prakrit—a language that had sounded to my ears like a baby's lisp. The anger I'd felt then comes back to me when I realize what I have been doing all these years. I have been speaking Prakrit myself. (192-93)

The entire process of Jaya's self-realization and her final choice that she would no more accept the terms of life imposed on her, but will argue at every point, are the outcome of her realizing the essence of the Indian classics and religious scriptures.[5] That is why Jaya cannot be angry with anybody but herself. If she would have acquired sufficient self-knowledge beforehand and would not bother about her safety, she could not be subdued by anybody. With this knowledge she cannot forgive herself, and therefore stops blaming others.

Shashi Deshpande's insight into the complex texture of Indian (Hindu) society is clear from her novel. She notes the existence of two simultaneous trends that had been prevailing in the Indian society since the days of the Puranas: there is a long tradition of worshipping goddesses, and also the tradition of denying human status to women. Again, women are not treated equally under the same roof. In a family the mother figure may be all-powerful while her daughters-in-law are tortured and humiliated. Such keen observation of reality enabled Deshpande to develop an unbiased view of the situation. The novel exposes her belief that the women themselves are not less responsible than men for the sufferings of the women. This belief held her from being a radical feminist. In fact, Indian soil is not fit for the kind of protest we find in some Western novels. Both men and women in India have to broaden their consciousness first, and to criticize their own feelings and attitudes in order to give equal status to women. Deshpande realized this fact and expressed it in her novel.

NOTES

1. Kim Chernin, *Reinventing Eve: Modern Woman in Search of Herself (*New York: Time Books, 1987), p. 176.
2. To quote G.S. Balarama Gupta, Deshpande's protagonists are "creatures of conventional morality: they are the ones who are unfairly abused, misused and ill-used. But they believe in conformity and compromise for the sake of retention of domestic harmony rather than revolt which might result in the disruption of familial concord." 'Indian English Women Short Story Writers: An Overview,' *Vikraam Journal of English Studies,* Vol. 1, p. 39
3. *Ibid.*
4. Jaya's relationship with Kamat, whom she left at his death-bed when the man stretched his hand towards her in utter loneliness and fear for death, may be interpreted in terms of her selfishness. The situation is also a typical Indian one. A married lady in India, particularly one who is devoted to the assumed role of 'Seeta,' is not expected to come close to another man in his need, even if she has needed his help and support. As Jaya says, "Kamat had been the only one I'd talked to about them [her rejected stories]. I'd had to tell him because I had needed him." (146) Yet, she left him during his 'need,' though there was an urge inside her to respond to his call. Jaya explains that she could not respond to his call as she faced the necessity to be someone else other than Mohan's wife, and she did not dare to accept reality, choosing to be an individual with many-faced personality. "'Jaya' he had said and I had become only Jaya. It had annihilated Mohan entirely." (157) While recounting the experience, she acknowledges that she felt like responding to Kamat's call. "There had been nothing but an overwhelming urge to respond to him with my body, the equally overwhelming certainty of my mind that I could not do so." (157) Though Jaya's mind and body were prepared for the union, her rational mind opposed to such union in order to safeguard her marriage. The man-woman relationship goes by the name of society in India. And people are not even conscious that they are lying to themselves while preferring to go by the dictates of society.

Jaya understood the gravity of her sin when Mukta accused her: "why did you leave him alone the day he died? You left him to die alone, didn't you?" (185) Jaya says: "The loneliness of a man facing his death—is there anything like it in this world? His pain filled the room and we both of us feel it, Mukta and I." (186) Both Jaya and Mukta were the victims of the Indian (Hindu) tradition that upholds the myth of Sita and hardly allows a married woman and even a widow (like Mukta) to come close to another man. "I suddenly realized—it was not Mohan but marriage that had made me circumspect." (187) Deshpande's keen observation of the trends in the Indian society that mould the characters becomes evident.

5. Dr. Sarvepalli Radhakrishnan expressed his view in regard to the influence of the great classics on one's life. As he observed in his *The Present Crisis of Faith,* great classics of our country can change the very character of the individual and the nature of the society. That Jaya's mind is drawing sustenance from the great literature of the world, is evident in the novel. As she reflects on her lack of real experiences of suffering, "Like the Chorus of Greek drama, we were distanced from suffering; for us, there was just living—one foot in front of another, until death came to us in a natural form." (4) While commenting on her conjugal relationship, Jaya says, "Sometimes, like the time I read an American poet's confession of her guilt because she just could not get along without her husband, it had seemed hopeless—I would never be able to shake off this monstrous burden." (97) The novel is strewn with such references to literature showing how Jaya has been moulded by the works of great writers.

Images and Symbols in *That Long Silence*

Figurative language is an essential part of poetry. Robert Frost liked to define poetry as metaphor, saying one thing in terms of another. An opposite view also developed in the twentieth century which provoked Ogden Nash to the sardonic comment: "One thing that literature would be greatly the better for would be a more restricted employment by authors of simile and metaphor."

The poets hardly avoid similes and metaphors. Even the novelists use them profusely. With a serious writer figurative language is never a decoration, but a means of exposing his/her points of view. Shashi Deshpande's *That Long Silence* is an example of her perfect use of figurative language for clarifying her ideas.

The novel is written in the form of retrospection by its protagonist Jaya, herself a writer. She starts with her difficulty in finding appropriate words and the strain reminds her of the process of childbirth—of fear of losing control over her own body. The comparison is suggestive of a particular suffering that women alone can go through. The protagonist soon clarifies why the letters are not coming out of her pen smoothly: she is engaged in self-revelation, writing of her husband Mohan and herself. "Self-revelation is a cruel process. The real picture, the real 'you' never emerges. Looking for it is as bewildering as trying to know how you really look. Ten different mirrors show you ten different faces." (1) As different mirrors may be used for getting different views of one's face, so interactions with different characters are introduced in the novel for exposing different selves of the protagonist. Even when she knows that the mirror is treacherous, that it "shows you only what you want to see," she is hankering after her views in mirror. Knowing that her self-portrait may be deceiving, she yet tries it.

Briefly speaking, the novel centres on man-woman relationship. In order to explain the traditional view of husband-wife relationship the novelist uses two popular similes—that of two bullocks tied together, and that of a sheltering tree. The image of two bullocks tied together is a typical Indian one, and when a married couple is compared to a pair of such bullocks, it suggests a lot about the concept of marriage in Indian society. There is a sense of compulsion and of mechanical movement: just as the tied bullocks cannot move separately, so are the husband and wife denied free movement. Or, rather, as is the custom, the wife is compelled to follow her husband without grumble. In the case of the bullocks they are whipped if they attempt to move separately. In the case of the husband and the wife, the Indian society is not permissive; particularly, a woman is always frowned upon by the society if she attempts to go astray. Mechanical movement is the common quality in this comparison. At the beginning of her married life, Jaya accepted this comparison as she had little moral courage then. She went to the Dadar flat with Mohan, following the footsteps of the mythical figures Sita and Draupadi. She did not ask her husband any question, and the image of two bullocks came to her mind automatically:

> A pair of bullocks yoked together . . . that was how I saw the two of us the day we came here. It was an eerie sensation I had whiling climbing up the stairs with him, as if there was for that one infinitesimal moment a pause in my being, and I, detached from my self, saw this . . . a pair of bullocks yoked together. (7)

In the silence of the Dadar flat, after Jaya was shocked at Mohan's accusations that he had been involved in business malpractice only to meet her demands, she starts serious introspection and her views begin to change. She acquires sufficient moral courage to make a free choice and asserts as an individual. To express her changed concept, she again goes back to the bullock image:

> A pair of bullocks yoked together . . . a clever phrase, but can it substitute for the reality? A man and a woman married for seventeen years. A couple with two children. A family somewhat like the one caught and preserved for posterity by the advertising visuals I so loved. But the reality was only this. We were two persons. A man. A woman. (8)

Jaya's changed sensibilities have enabled her to acknowledge that she too is a separate person who can exercise her freedom to deviate from the way of her husband. Hence, the two bullocks tied together would not be a fitting symbol for them. Deshpande has thus exploited the symbol of the bullocks, using it both from the negative and the positive points of view.

Besides the image of the bullocks, the image of the sheltering tree is also repeatedly introduced in the novel for describing the relationship between the husband and her wife in the Indian context. Jaya's Vanitamami told her as an advice that Jaya should treat her husband as a sheltering tree. She also told that one should not bother even if her husband has a mistress. She should rather develop some hobbies such as keeping cats. Vanitamami's own life is a miserable instance of tolerating humiliations from her in-laws, and yet she continued to support her husband lest she be shelter-less. Moreover, she was childless, and that increased her suffering. Everywhere in India the picture is more or less the same. Be the woman a maidservant trailing from door to door or a happy housewife with husband in good job, she has to water the 'sheltering tree' to keep it alive so that she may put on 'kumkum' on her forehead. What if the husband is a drunkard and beats her regularly or a suspicious brute that makes her life hell. It is necessary to keep him alive. Thus the maidservant Jeeja scolds Tara when the latter, out of despair and frustration, wishes her husband's death. Jeeja reminds her that Tara can still use 'kumkum' on her forehead only because her husband Rajaram is still surviving. What is a woman who is denied 'kumkum'?—she says. And when Rajaram is stabbed, these two poor women try their best to get him cured. What else could be a better metaphor than 'husband is a sheltering tree' to render Tara's feelings towards Rajaram?

Even Jaya also, before she started introspection, accepted Mohan as a sheltering tree. That is why she never questioned him, knowing that he may be angry with her and she may lose her sheltered existence. During their stay in Dadar flat when there was little romance of married life left for her,[1] she could not be harsh towards her. "Even if I could no longer call it love, the emotion that governed my behaviour to him, there was still the habit of being a wife, of sustaining and supporting him, that made cruelty to him impossible. And a habit is something that is infinitely more difficult to get rid of." (98) When Mohan left the Dadar flat leaving Jaya alone, she did not know what to do alone. On Jeeja's request she had to go to the hospital where she met Dr. Vyas who happened to be her brother's friend. She requested him to take care of Jeeja's step-son and he assured her, and then asked her to drop in at his residence with her husband. After leaving him Jaya reflects on his possible reactions if he learns that Mohan has left her.

> 'With your husband of course'—what did he mean by that? Was it impossible for me to relate to the world without Mohan? A husband is like a sheltering tree. . . . Vanitamami, did you, without knowing it, speak the most profound truth I'm destined to hear in my life? What would he have done if I'd told him Mohan has left me? How would he have looked at me then? With pity? Contempt? Or, most frightening thought, without that barrier Mohan had raised between me and other men? (167)

Jaya's reflections show the impact of Vanitamami's words on her mind.

It was her fear, she acknowledges later, that held her from accepting the reality. However, the metaphor of the sheltering tree aptly reveals an Indian woman's attitude to her husband. When an enlightened woman tries to emerge out of this age-old concept—as Jaya does in *That Long Silence'*— she has to struggle hard with her self. For it is her internal fear that stands on the way of a woman's self-actualization. In order to assert her individuality, a woman is required to justify the implications of such age-old concepts as 'husband is the sheltering tree.' Deshpande's success lies in her use of symbols and images which help to highlight the theme of the novel.

After Mohan had been accused of misappropriation of money and investigation against him had started, he was apprehending loss of job and humiliation. At that time he once asked Jaya if she remembered the incident of the Nair. Nair was also accused of a similar case, and being desperate the entire family committed suicide. Jaya remembered Nair and visualized the picture of their death. "I had seen the picture, not with the vagueness of a dream or the dimness of a fantasy, but with the clarity and exactness with which one sees a movie. All the details clear, larger than life and in Technicolor." (10) And this image helped her to visualize another, a picture of four of them—Mohan, Rahul, Rati and she herself—jointly venturing suicide. The picture appeared absurd and Jaya laughed at it:

> I had cringed then under Mohan's ridicule, but now I have to laugh at my own fantasy. Yes, it was absurd. Could we have come to such a decision without squabbling? We, who could not even decide upon a meal or a movie without bickering—could we have chosen death in such harmony?
>
> For Mohan, the thing had been far more simple. The idea was just plain stupid. The lemming drive, the death wish, is unknown to him. (10-11)

Image is used for sketching a character in the above passage. The device of image has been exploited to show the difference between the two characters—Jaya and Mohan. Jaya's imaginative flight as well as her sense of reality is exposed through her visualizing a picture of suicide jointly taken up by the entire family and then rejecting the possibility of such a venture. Here is a unique use of image for sketching characters in a novel.

Deshpande has developed a narrative style that depends largely on the figurative use of language. Take, for example, the description of the idle days spent by the couple in Dadar flat:

> We had drunk our tea, had our baths, and then the day rushed at us with all the savagery of a dog unleashed after too long. We looked at each other and found the same question in the other's eyes: what are we going to do with ourselves? It was not the larger conundrum of what we were to do with our lives that confronted us; it was a simple puzzle—what are we to do with ourselves this moment, this day, the next moment, the next day. (24)

Again, those days are compared to the time of waiting in a train that is ready for departure, but does not while other trains pass by it:

> It was like sitting in a stationary train. There is movement, bustle, noise all about you, your train is gathering speed, and you're off. Then the sudden shocking silence and the gleaming rails outside tell you it was the other train that has left, the other train that moved away. Your own movement has been only an illusion. You are right where you were all along. (24)

The anxieties of the couple who are waiting for the result of the investigation of the charge of malpractice brought against the husband, and have been compelled to leave their furnished flat to live a sort of exiled life in a small flat in a dull dingy part of the metropolis, could not be better expressed otherwise. The same concern is expressed through the reference to a nursery rhyme used by children while moving around a tree:

'What's that song the children used to sing when they were little? . . . I think it was some sort of a game . . . something about a mulberry bush?'

'Here we go round the mulberry bush'?

'Yes, that's the one.' And seeing my enquiring gaze fixed on his face, he said lamely, 'I just thought of that song, I don't know why.'

> Now, I can hazard a guess as to the trend of his thoughts. You imagine you're moving, getting on, going ahead, but actually you're just going round and round, coming to the same point over and over again. But, if my conjecture is right, to what point in his life was he connecting his situation? Maybe it was not his life, our life together that he was thinking of (33)

The symbol of moving around a mulberry bush is suggestive of a lack of a goal in life. Excessively attached to materialism, Mohan has always been trying to get more and more material comforts at the cost of losing real values of life. As Jaya says,

> It was as if . . . Mohan had realized that he had moved, after years of struggle, only from not having enough money for clothes, fees and books, to not having enough for a gas connection, for travelling in comfort, for his brother's clothes, his sister's fees. (60)

Jaya's evaluation of Mohan's character serves as an illustration of the symbol of mulberry bush used in the novel. Blinded by the glamour of comforts most of the people in the modern world rush for more and more material gain without bothering about any ethical concern. And as a result, it is ultimately revealed that there was actually no progress in their lives; they have been only moving around the same place.

Deshpande has also used dreams as symbols. Jaya's dream of being left alone by her companion is not just an indication of a future incident of Mohan's leaving the Dadar flat without telling her anything. It is her psychological alienation from others, and particularly Mohan, that is suggested through her dream. In the dream that she had during her stay with Mohan in the Dadar flat, she was first walking along with her companion ('we were walking together') between rows of houses, "so close to one another that there is a slight sense of claustrophobia." Suddenly she found her alone, after climbing 'the flight of stairs' with much struggle and with the help of a girl. The revelation that she was alone came upon her with a sense of shock. "The realization that I am lost overwhelms me. Worse—I do not know where I am, where I have to go and how I can find him. The orientation is total." (86) She found herself surrounded by a number of young girls who were all smiling. Suddenly, a thought came to her that the girls were on her side, but none of them could help her. She felt utterly helpless and ill. As she lay down, stiff as a corpse, the faces around her changed from curiosity to sympathy. As she continued to lie there, paralyzed and aphasic, the girls were discussing her predicament, talking in low tones among themselves.

At that time her companion (Jaya refers to the companion as 'he,' and not as Mohan) came in a hurry and told that a taxi was waiting for them near the Portuguese Church and they would have to run for it. Immediately she started running after him, but felt that she was already late and they would never be able to go away. And it was for her fault. With this realization she woke up and remembered how her elder brother never accepted the existence of truth in a dream. She also tried to neglect the dream, but was not sure if it contained some truth in it. But for the readers, the dream is a reflection of the interior part of her mind—maybe the subconscious or the unconscious self—of which she is yet to be aware. By now, Jaya is sure that she is not going to write for the column of Seeta; she is now eager to write about the real problems faced by Indian women. But the process of her self-realization is not yet complete. She feels that her way has been deviated from Mohan's, and yet she is afraid of the prospect of remaining alone. Her fear for being alienated is symbolized by the dream. The girls in the dream, who treat her sympathetically, may be possible characters in her book that she is trying to write.

She is now almost at the end of the process of self-realization, but has to face some other facts boldly. The dream reveals a state of confusion which is due mainly to her fear. Two more incidents—that of Mohan's leaving the Dadar flat leaving her alone, and the accusation brought against her (by Mukta) that she had left Kamat to die alone—will accelerate the process of her self-realization, and she is expected to find out her destination as a writer and as an individual. The dream reveals that she has not yet reached that stage.

Deshpande has also used metaphor and simile to express a particular mood of her characters. When Mohan accused Jaya of isolating herself from him and his concern, and also of not caring about the children, her 'feeble defences' had no chance before Mohan's 'fierce onslaughts.' She tried her best to stop him with counter-attack, but failed. She thought that "real bitterness clawed its way through this self-mockery," and returned to her silence. In order to express her suppressed anger she takes the help of an image:

> But nothing could stop him. It was like a deluge. Ramukaka's Meera, who had been in Poona the year the Panshet Dam had burst, had told us how, hearing that the river was rising, some of them had gone, filled with pleasurable excitement, to see it. 'But the river was rising, was rising so fast, we had to run back. It was as if it was chasing us. A few minutes more and we could have been drowned.' There had been incredulous anger in her tone, the angry amazement of one betrayed by something she had thought innocuous.
>
> I felt the same now. 'Cheating, cheating' I wanted to cry out, the way we had as children when we knew we were going to be cheated. But as if I'd been struck dumb, I could say nothing. I sat in my place, pinned to it by his anger, a monstrously huge spear that went through me, excruciatingly painful, yet leaving me cruelly conscious. (120-21)

One may remember, in this context, the lines in Eliot's 'The Love Song of J. Alfred Prufrock':

> And when I am formulated, sprawling on a pin,
> When I am pinned and wriggling on the wall,
> Then how should I begin
> To spit out all the butt-ends of my days and ways?

Jaya's suffering, like Prufrock's, is better expressed through metaphors. Her silence is often due to her sensitiveness; she just does not know how she should begin arguing with someone who hardly understands her language. Her inexpressible suffering is thus poetically rendered by the author.

Jaya's relationship with Kamat is rendered through suggestions. She wonders why Kamat enters every now and then in the story of her married life, but she cannot help it. She is yet to acknowledge to herself her true relationship with Kamat. Whenever she faced any crisis—be it her father's death, or the rejection of her stories by the publishers, or the success of the Seeta column—she rushed to Kamat for comfort or for sharing feelings. Their relationship is never defined, but only hinted at. Some extracts from their conversations may be quoted:

> 'The fact is' he has gone on, 'I don't want to concede to any woman power over me. Sex . . . yes, that's one area where I do concede that power. But nowhere else.' (152)
>
> Another time he'd said, 'I like my women thin. . . . I prefer clean, spare lines in a human being. You, for example.' It was then that he had said to me, 'Your name is like your face.' (152)
>
> It was becoming difficult—the more I thought of him, the more complicated his character seemed; the more I tried to put the pieces together, the less possible it became to see the shape of our relationship. Love? But what did I know of love? Even the love stories I'd written—they had been as if fantasies of my adolescence. Love? No, I knew nothing of it (153)

Though Jaya repeatedly denies that theirs was no love relationship, it is suggested that their relationship may not be explained with some other words. Curiously enough, Jaya describes the dead body of Kamat in such a way that there is hardly any scope for the readers to assume that Jaya actually visualized the scene. Only after Mukta tells her that had she not been there, Kamat's dead body would remain in the closed flat, the readers come to know that Jaya only saw a hallucination.[2] Jaya says,

> I had gone back some days later. I had gone not knowing why I was going or what I was going to say to him. I had climbed up the stairs, mechanically counting them as I had always done, feeling as if time had frozen since I had turned away from him, and he would be waiting for me still, the same pose, hands fallen at sides, the same look on his face. But I had found him dead—glassy-eyed, foul-smelling and dead—and I had walked away from him. (157)

The description of "glassy-eyed, foul-smelling" dead body, an imaginary one, is used for depicting the impact of Kamat's death on Jaya. Here is, again, another unique use of images for delving deep beneath the surface of the mind.

That Long Silence reveals its author's hold on the use of symbols and imagery for tracing the evolution of Jaya's consciousness. Some critics even argue that the novelist is dealing in abstractions and not in physical detail.[3] From such a point of view, Mohan and Jaya are only concepts and the whole exercise is based on the struggle between these two forces "tending to acquire different significations in different situations."[4] But if the characters are treated as abstractions, the novelist would be denied a hold on characterization, a hold that marks her distinctness. Finally, Deshpande has also used folktale as a symbol. Jaya finds symbolic significance in the tale of crow and sparrow told by her mother in childhood, and realizes the message for every housewife contained therein. The sparrow in the tale symbolizes a housewife who is busy with her kids and family hazards, and hardly bothers about the outer world. The crow is the symbol of foolhardiness and simplicity that is killed when after a long waiting in the rain outside he is allowed to enter the sparrow's wax-built nest, but is deluded to sit on a hot stove for getting him warm. Jaya deduces the inner meaning of the tale:

> There's the foolish, improvident, irresponsible, gullible crow; and there's the cautious, self-centred, worldly-wise, dutiful, shrewd sparrow. The survivor is the sparrow, the sparrow who keeps the crow waiting for hours, and finally, in the guise of providing sympathy and shelter, kills the crow. . . . They [little girls] will store this story in their subconscious, their unconscious or whatever, and eventually they will become that damnably, insufferably priggish sparrow looking after their homes, their babies . . . and to hell with the rest of the world. Stay at home, look after your babies, keep out the rest of the world and you're safe. (17)

In fact, Deshpande aims her lash of satire towards the selfish house wives who manage a life of comfort for themselves and have least concern for others' suffering. Through the change in Jaya's consciousness, the novelist's ideas are delivered. The unique way of using symbols enabled her ideas to be rendered artistically.

NOTES

1. Quite naturally, Jaya felt physical attraction towards Mohan just after their marriage. But gradually she developed the notion that the physical contact is illusory. "Man and woman—it was then that I realized the deep chasm between the two. They are separated for ever, never more than at the moment of total physical togetherness." (98)
2. Mukta says to Jaya, "Then why did you leave him [Kamat] alone the day he died? You left him to die alone, didn't you? I saw you go up to his house that day, I heard you come down, and when I went up a little later, he was dead. You let him die alone, didn't you? Why did you do it, Jaya, why did you?"
3. In his article "The Indian Woman Writer's Angle," Suresh Chandra observes with reference to *That Long Silence*, "In her struggle to break free of various imprisoning social and domestic

structures, she realizes that each object, whether animate or inanimate, is an obstacle not because of its physical presence but because of its semiotic dimensions calling for a certain combination of signifiers. . . . The major characters of Mohan and Jaya are only concepts. . . . Mohan is not a character but a concept whose chief attribute is slipperiness. . . . Jaya is that who conquers and surmounts all obstacles, all allurements and sees through the mists of illusions and temptations. To be a Jaya it is imperative to be enlightened—*atta deepo bhab*—so as to able to fight the darkness of ignorance, illusion and temptation." *Essays in Comparative Literature* (New Delhi; Anmol, 1998), pp. 35-36.

4. S. Gill, *Abelardian Semiotics*, p. 23, Qtd. Suresh Chandra, *Essays in Comparative Literature*, p. 35.

Conclusion

That Long Silence being a novel by a woman writer and its protagonist being a woman, who rejects her previous approach to life and art to emerge as a self-conscious realist through her writings, draws a special attention of the feminists. It may not be surprising if some critics compare the novel with similar works of some western writers and find 'distortions of female experience' in her writings. For, the protagonist Jaya in *That Long Silence* hardly resembles the typical women figures in the writings of the western feminists—the women who always protest and never compromise, and thanks to these qualities, are accepted as the epitome of feminism. Commenting on this trend of some Canadian critics who find fault with the women characters in the writings of McLennan, Callaghan and Davies, Margaret Atwood said: "A feminist criticism is emerging, I've read at least one review, and I'm sure there have been and will be more, in which a novelist was criticized for not having made her heroine's life different, even though that life was more typical of the average woman's life in this society than the reviewer's 'liberated' version would have been. Perhaps Women's Lib reviewers will start demanding that heroines resolve their difficulties with husband, kids, or themselves by stomping out to join a consciousness raising group, which will be no more satisfactory from the point of view of literature than the legendary Socialist Realist romance with one's tractor."[1] This ironic remark by Atwood may as well be applied in defence of Shashi Deshpande's novels where the women characters are seen compromising with the terms of life.

Jaya in *That Long Silence* hardly protests. She did not protest when Mohan said that anger makes a woman unwomanly. She did not take up Kamat's advice who told her to express anger in her writings. She also did not go against Mohan's will when Mohan opposed the idea of her joining a rally, or adopting a baby, or even taking a job. She even did not accuse Mohan of bringing disrepute to the family by his malpractice. Rather Mohan brought the charge that she had little concern for his 'difficulties,' and that whatever he did was meant for Jaya and her children. Surprisingly, Jaya did not express her anger even then. And when Mohan left the Dadar flat leaving her alone, she became panicky with the thought of being lonely. And lastly when everything becomes as before, she does not take a strong decision to teach Mohan a good lesson. She just decides to break her silence and to compel Mohan to listen to her:

> Mohan will be back. 'All well' his telegram says. Does he mean by this that we will go back to being 'as we were'? Does it mean that, now that Mohan has sorted out his problem, and no longer fears prosecution, joblessness and disgrace, we can go back to our original positions? Does it mean that he will come back and give me a carefully edited version of what has happened—as he has done so often till now—and then ask me, 'What do you say, Jaya?'
>
> Until today, this has been a rhetorical question. I have looked at his face for clues and then given the answer I know he wants. I have only to do this now and authority will seep into Mohan once more.
>
> But it is no longer possible for me. If I have to plug that 'hole in the heart,' I will have to speak, to listen, I will have to erase the silence between us. (192)

With this attitude of Jaya, the radical feminists have every reason to be dissatisfied. For, Jaya hardly conforms to the modern concept of the emancipation of women, the concept that came in vogue with Ibsen's *A Doll's House*.

Jaya's attitude has to be understood from an existentialist's point of view who is true to herself. Her acute self-conscious and keen observations make it clear to her that she cannot avoid her responsibility. She could exercise her power if she had 'chosen' it—or to be more specific, if she could have removed fear from her mind. She had been excessively attached to a sheltered life, and was afraid to take any risk. To abide by Mohan's will assured a cosy, peaceful life, and at the cost of this comfort she was not ready to assert her individuality. 'With this knowledge what forgiveness?' She cannot forgive her for her lack of courage. In a typical Indian way—Gandhiji also followed the path of scrutinizing himself —Jaya first analyzed her own self, and then understood that the future depends on her own action. If she would leave Mohan and start living on her own, she could be able to maintain her well but Mohan continued to remain a threat to society. Jaya's decision that she would henceforward argue with Mohan raises a hope that her future course may change Mohan's attitude.

Jaya's acute ethical sense, which was earlier subdued by her own fear, does not allow her to think in the line of the feminist thinkers. She accepts it to be her duty to argue with Mohan on every issue so that he would no more get an easy way of escape. She remembers that Mohan has always been in the habit of asking Jaya's opinion on everything, and she developed the habit of giving him consent just to avoid any tussle with him. She now feels that Mohan has taken her for granted only because of her own behaviour. Though she knows that human nature cannot be easily changed, she will at least try for bringing some change in Mohan's character so that he may develop ethical sense and may accept his own responsibility for the work done by her. Jaya was stunned by Mohan's callous remark on the charge of malpractice brought against him.

> 'We don't have to go to extremes,' he had said to me with pedantic dryness. 'Nair was a fool, he left himself too wide open. He was greedy for money. . . . I've just accepted a few favours from people I know. Things are not too bad, I'm not that involved. Agarwal—I don't know how Agarwal slipped, he was always very careful. But this time. . . this man whose tender was rejected, he's related to the Minister, that was bad luck, the Minister is new, and Agarwal didn't know him well. He's trying to meet him now, to get the inquiry put off.' (11)

Jaya did not protest when she heard Mohan explain his 'problem' casually. With her changed sensibilities, she feels the gravity of her sin when she remained silent even at this shameless show. She wants to change the course of her action now, though she knows that it is indeed hard to change anybody's nature.

Moreover, Jaya has developed a total understanding of Mohan's character, and because of this understanding she started pitying him even when he flared up in anger. She knew that anger was used as protection by him, and this realization held her back from showing a counter anger. Jaya also understood that Mohan's past contained some incidents which he disowns, as he is unable to tolerate the humiliation attached to those facts. His mother's being a cook is one such incident. She can also feel the timidity and humiliation of young Mohan who had to join a wedding feast only to obey his old patron's order. Jaya can study his mind clearly and knows all his limitations. She also knows that there are women like her two 'ajjis' who could control their families, and like her mother who never obeyed her husband. She was astonished to know that Jaya had cut her long hair only to obey Mohan. And yet she never tried to control her husband as it did not suit her temperament. Actually, she has no faith in the art of controlling others. But she made a mistake in her relationship with Mohan. She should have observed the pattern of his work in office—she should have tried to know the nature of the machinery that got him transferred or supplied him with a better quarter—and then she could somehow check his moral lapse. Jaya perhaps recalls the saying that both the sinner and the person who does not protest against sin, are equally treated by god. Hence she finds no valid reason of being seriously angry with Mohan. The nature of Jaya's realization renders her 'not fit' for the role of a feminist. But her human feelings are highlighted by the author.

NOTE

1. Margaret Atwood, "Paradoxes and Dilemmas: On Being a Woman Writer," *Second Words* (Toronto: McClelland & Stewart, 1982), p. 192.